Lincolnics; familiar sayings of Abraham Lincoln

Henry Llewellyn Williams, Abraham Lincoln

Abraham Lincoln

From the photograph by Rice. Copyright, 1901
by Gilbo & Co., New York

Lincolnics

Familiar Sayings of Abraham Lincoln

Collected and Edited by

Henry Llewellyn Williams

New York and London

G. P. Putnam's Sons

The Knickerbocker Press

PREFACE.

"To rule people," (says Professor ,ittré) "there is not so much need to :now what they have done or are doing, .s what they think and how they say it." t would, therefore, be better to be the 'oice of the people than their law-giver ›r their song-writer.

· Lincoln had many difficulties to cont end with in his early attempts as an orator.· He faced backwoods hearers, he had o pierce dulness, ignorance, narrowness, .nd intellectual blindness. His thoughts vere purely his own, but he was forced o couch them in everyday speech—to use he tongue of the common people. His ›oints, proofs, images, reasoning, truisms were taken from the familiar facts of daily life, but, being wrought upon by h' own personal qualities and spirit of i dependence, they became clear, compa forceful, and convincing—a foil is bu an iron rod, but becomes a sword in the hand of a fencing master.

Lincoln's Presidential speeches, when read aloud, or compared with the finest literary efforts, show clearly that he gained his secret spell from the great prose writers. Any man in the crowd could read out the Gettysburg address and all the others would catch the meaning and feel the mere melodious charm. The foreigner might thus make Lincoln intelligible, while Adams, Everett, or even Webster, not to say Choate, would be discordant or perplexing.

Lincoln proved that eloquence neec not be born aristocratic or college brea Though commonplace, his similes were nevertheless satisfying, explicit, and cogent,—plain but potent.

A German legend avers that a treasure

buried in the Rhine will float up when the Right Word is spoken. Lincoln was the Magician who always spoke the Right Word, and treasures of valor, devotion, and loyalty were forthcoming in consequence thereof. His call to arms brought thousands in review before "Father Abraham," and his word sent them to "charge with a smile." His reference to the "weeping widows" and "mourning households," when the gigantic fraternal duel was ended and victor and vanquished wished to unite to drive the usurper from Mexico, quelled the warlike spirit, opened the clenched fist, and folded it in prayer.

Montesquieu has said, "Illuminate history by laws"—Abraham Lincoln irradiated the history of our country by scintillations of his wit, wisdom, and trenchant satire, despite the thundercloud threatening to be the pall of American ambition, prosperity, and brotherhood.

His speeches, addresses, proclamations were for the hosts and multitudes; his sayings were spoken to the individual. In youth he taught, and entertained his rude fellows, and set them examples; as a lawyer, he counselled the simple and righted the injured widow and orphan. On the eve of his inauguration, he delays to bid farewell to his parents; at the height of the war, he reads the wounded into the last sleep from his mother's Bible. At his receptions, he passes by the office-seeker to say a pleasantry to the humble petitioner, and men were prouder that they had cracked jokes or split rails with "Honest Old Abe" than were those who had split hairs with him in Cabinet councils.

The reader of this collection will certainly cry out with the man who heard Shakespeare for the first time on the stage: "How full of quotations!" for few books and periodicals but have pointed a moral and adorned a tale with a *Lincolnic.*

Never abstruse. far-fetched, or complex, "plain as a pike staff" and as penetrative, this colloquially delightful epigrammatist offers sentences apt and terse, pregnant with meaning, and "handy to have about the house" as "Mr. Toodles" says. They form a sensible "constant companion," a perpetual fount of pertinent application, relief, or inspiration for the desk, the lecture-stand, the rostrum, and even the pulpit, for our martyred chief backed his patriotism with piety.

To the life of Washington, Lincoln ascribed a great formative influence upon his own life and character. May it be said of the sayings of Lincoln that they have helped to "set the foot in the right place" towards the upbuilding of character and true patriotism.

THE EDITOR.

YEAR		
1809	Feb. 12	Abraham Lincoln born. (Hardin) Larue County, Ky.
		Note:—President Jefferson's second term expires; succeeded by James Madison for two terms also, until 1817.
1813		Lincoln family moves to Knob Creek; Abraham, aged five,
1816		nearly drowns. Father, mother, Abraham, and sister, move into Indiana; settle at "Gooseneck," Pigeon Creek's Bend, near Charleston; store, Gentryville, Perry (now Spencer) County; clearing and log-hut.
1817		Indiana added to the Union.
1818		James Monroe, President.
		Illinois added to the Union. Lincoln, by mother's tuition, writes his name in the Family Bible. Mother (Nancy
1819		Hanks) dies. Abraham writes his first letter, for the funeral. Lincoln's father, Thomas, marries—second time—Mrs.
1820		Sarah Johnson (Johnston), widow with three children.
1823		"The Missouri Compromise."
1825		The Monroe Doctrine proclaimed.
		John Quincy Adams, President; Calhoun, Vice-President for two terms.

1826		Lincoln, ferryman on Ohio River.
	July 4	Deaths, same day, ex-Presidents John Adams and Thomas Jefferson.
		Lincoln at miscellaneous farm work; reads. studies, visits county courts; publishes, locally, articles on Temperance and on Politics.
1827		Builds a flatboat and takes home-produce to New Orleans.
1828		Takes flatboat to New Orleans, sells it and freight, returns on steamboat.
1829		Andrew Jackson, President for two terms.
1830	Feb.–Mar.	Lincoln family remove to Macon (not Mason) County, Ill.; loghouse, near Decatur, Sangamon River.
		Abraham of age, works independently; makes 3000 fence-rails under contract.
1831		Builds flatboat, takes it laden to sell at New Orleans; sees slave sales there. His employer, Denton Offutt (sometimes Thomas Affut), being pleased, offers him a clerkship in his store at New Salem. Lincoln leaves a saw-mill managership for it.
	July	Buys store and stock, enters into partnership with one Berry.

1832	March 9	Lincoln's first political address.
	Aug. 6	Locally successful; defeated for General Assemblyman. Returns to business.
	Sept. 20	Clerk of Elections at New Salem.
		Clerk at grocery-store; attends debating clubs; pilots a steamboat up Sangamon River to test navigability; studies grammar; makes acquaintance of Richard Yates (War-Governor of Illinois); fails as store-keeper; in debt.
	July–Aug.	"Black Hawk" War: Lincoln, Captain Illinois Mounted Rangers, mustered in by Lieut. Zachary Taylor (later General and President). In the same war, were Lieut. Jefferson C. Davis (afterwards President C. S. of A.), and Lieut. Robert Anderson (Major commanding Fort Sumter). In the new levy, Lincoln was private in the Illinois Volunteers.
1833		"Hired out" to any labor; intended apprenticeship to blacksmithing.
	May 7	Post-master of New Salem. Reads, local papers—Cincinnati *Gazette*, Louisville *Journal*, Mississippi *Republican*. Reads Gibbon, Rollin, Volney, Burns, Paine, Shakespeare, making notes and committing to memory. Studies Euclid to become land surveyor (profitably).

1834	Elected to State Legislature (2 years' term) as a (Henry) "Clay" man, opposed to the (Andrew) "Jackson" man; a Whig, but the local Democrats voted for him. He was a silent member and not even a "Single-speech Hamilton."
1835	Death of Lincoln's betrothed, Miss Ann (or Anne) Rutledge, at New Salem. Lincoln deeply grieved.
1836	Re-elected to Legislature. S. A. Douglas, Baker, Hardin, in the House. Lincoln's speeches attract notice; he is ranked with the Abolitionists; protests against Pro-slavery motions. All the nine Sangamon members being tall, were called "The Long Nine" (a cigar term), Lincoln being tallest. He induced change of Government seat from Vandalia to Springfield.
1837	Martin Van Buren, President till 1841. Lincoln had his acquaintance.
	Lincoln buys a house and lot on 8th Street, Springfield; has furniture made to suit his stature. Law license taken out; law partnership with John T. Stuart. Lectures in Springfield.
1838	Re-elected to Illinois Legislature (3d term); expenses 75 cts. (for cider); large majority.

1839	Dec.	Admitted to U. S. Circuit Courts.
1840		Pays final due old store bankrupt debt. General nickname "Honest Old Abe." Re-elected to State Legislature. Dissolves partnership with J. T. Stuart to enter into one with Judge S. T. Logan.
1841		William H. Harrison, President, died one month after inauguration; succeeded by the Vice-President, John Tyler.
1842		Lincoln enlists in the Temperance movement, in the "Washingtonians"; delivers addresses in Springfield. Whig County Convention, at primary, chose Abraham Lincoln and two others as delegates to nominate a Congressional candidate. For both his colleagues Lincoln waived his claims and they entered Congress before him.
1844		Lincoln composes poetry. As Presidential *elector*, he makes "Clay and Polk" campaign speeches in Illinois and Indiana.
1845		Dissolves law-partnership with Judge Logan to enter into one with W. H. Herndon.
1846		Elected Member of Congress, the one Whig from his State. Opposed to the popular Mexican War.
1847	Nov.	After Gen. Taylor's election for President, Lincoln introduced a bill in Congress considering emancipation of slaves in the District of Columbia.

1848	Dec.	Introduces "the Spot" resolutions against the Mexican War. Declines re-election to Congress. In contact in Washington with J. Q. Adams, Webster, Winthrop, Benton, President Buchanan, Douglas, Toombs, Andrew Johnson, A. H. Stephens, Jeff. C. Davis (Senate), "Long John" Wentworth, etc.
1849	March 5	(The 4th was Sunday.) Gen. Zach. Taylor, President. Lincoln's term out; applies for Land Commissionership, but is forestalled; refuses Oregon Territory Governorship; returns to Springfield to widen his law practice; (Major) Ellsworth of "the Chicago Zouaves" his law-student clerk.
1850	July 9	President Taylor died; succeeded by Vice-President Millard Fillmore. Abolition of slavery in District of Columbia. "The Fugitive Slave Law" repealed.
1851	Jan. 17	Thomas Lincoln (Abraham's father) dies in Coles County, Ill., twenty years' resident.
1852		Lincoln delivers a funeral eulogy on Henry Clay; speeches for Gen. Winfield Scott; addresses on Temperance.
1853	March 4	Franklin Pierce, President. Lincoln, attorney to Illinois Central R. R. Company; bill for services $1000 less retainer $250. Supt. Geo. B. McClellan (afterwards General-in-

		Chief U. S. A.) defers payment, alleging: "That is as much as a first-class lawyer would claim."
1854		"The Missouri Compromise" Act repealed. Civil War in Kansas (Territory). "Ossawatomie" John Brown in notice.
	January	"The Kansas-Nebraska" Bill excites passion. Lincoln comes out of his privacy to antagonize the Pro-slavery Party (Stephen A. Douglas, the oracle) in the North. Lincoln's family now consisted of three sons (one had died in infancy); his law practice remunerative.
1855		Speeches refuting Douglas. Elected to State Legislature; resigns to seek U. S. Senatorship, but defeated by Douglas, is re-elected.
1856	May	Held as leader of the Republican (formed on the "Free Soil") Party; it nominated J. C. Fremont and W. L. Dayton as President and Vice-President.
	May 29	Lincoln's speech at Bloomington Convention, generally considered "the greatest made in Illinois"; also regarded as "on the track for the Presidency."
	June 17	Pittsburg Republican National Convention: Abraham Lincoln 110 votes on the Vice-Presidency ballot. He was at Urbana attending court.

1857	March 4	James Buchanan (Dem.) and J. C. Breckenridge, President and Vice-President.
		The Dred Scott (fugitive slave) Supreme Court decision.
	June	Lincoln in speech, Springfield, deems the above erroneous.
1858		Illinois Republicans nominate Abraham Lincoln to the senatorship to be vacated by Douglas. "Our first and only choice."
	June	Speech, "The House Divided," splits the party: Douglas is re-elected. Their speeches comprised a challenge debate
	Aug–Oct.	in seven towns, drawing multitudes.
1859		Lincoln spoke in Ohio, Kansas, etc.
		John Brown's raid to cause a slaves' rising.
		Oregon admitted.
		Republican Convention.
1860	February	Lincoln tours New England, and at New York City is introduced to a mass-meeting at Cooper Institute by W. C. Bryant.
	Mar. 16-18	Chicago Republican Convention, unanimously nominated President; Hannibal Hamlin, Vice-President.
	Nov. 6	Abraham Lincoln elected President; $\frac{1,866,452}{1,857,610}$ votes; over

		Douglas, 491,634. Electoral College, 180; Douglas, 12. Votes cast: 4,682,069. Plurality, 18 to 46; a little over one-third. Population ratio; one voter to six and one-half.
	Dec. 20	South Carolina secedes from the Union.
	Dec. 28	Major Anderson evacuates Fort Moultrie, Charleston Harbor, and concentrates in Fort Sumter.
1861		Kansas added as a free State.
	January	Mississippi secedes; appoints Jefferson Davis (her senator) Commander-in-chief.
	Jan. 10	Supply steamer fired on and driven off from Charleston. Popular cry throughout the loyal States: "Our flag has been fired on. War!"
		Secession of Florida, Alabama, Georgia, Louisiana; Texas later.
	Feb. 4	The seceded States form, in a Congress, "the Confederate States of America." Jefferson Davis elected President;
	Feb. 19	inaugurated.
	Feb. 11	President-elect Abraham Lincoln visits his stepmother. Farewell to Springfield, sad, ominous. "We will pray for you!" the popular cry.
	Feb. 23	Lincoln surreptitiously enters Washington.

		Secession accepted as a fact.
1861	Mar. 4	Lincoln inaugurated.
		Secretaries of War and Treasury, Thompson and Floyd, displaced by Holt (Kentucky) *ante* Cameron, and Dix (New York) *ante* S. P. Chase.
	April 12	Fort Sumter fired upon.
	April 19	Baltimore riots against Volunteers passing through to garrison the capital.
	April 20	Union mass-meeting, at New York.
	May 3	President's Proclamation calling for 500,000 Volunteers for three years. From a timely verse "We are coming, *Father Abraham*," Lincoln retains that name. *Habeas Corpus* writ suspended.
	July 4	President's Message: calls for $410,000,000. Popular cry: "On to Richmond!"
	July 21	Bull Run battle. Federal repulse.
	August	General Fremont, in Missouri, frees slaves under a Confiscation Act; rebuked; his order modified by the President.
	Aug. 10	Wilson's Creek, Mo., defeat of Federals.
	September	National Fast Day in memory of Bull Run defeat.

1861	October	The President reviews 100,000 soldiers of the Army of the Potomac.
	Oct. 21	Ball's Bluff. Federal defeat.
	November	Confederate Commissioners Mason and Slidell taken off a British passenger-steamer and imprisoned at Boston; released after possible war with Great Britain. This kingdom pronounces the Confederate States of America's privateers belligerents.
	December	President angry at great army contract frauds; otherwise, calm and confident.
1862	January	Secretary of War Cameron replaced by Stanton.
	Jan. 30	Ericsson's iron-clad turret warship the *Monitor* launched at New York.
	February	President Lincoln's son Willie died in the White House.
	March	First iron-clad action: the *Merrimac*, Confederate ram, after sinking United States warships, is repulsed, disabled by the *Monitor*.
		The President, as acting Commander-in-chief, overrules Gen. McClellan and Council of War as to immediate forward movement.
		President's Message recommends joint Congress resolution

		to co-operate pecuniarily with any State gradually abolishing slavery.
1862	April	Act prohibiting slavery.
		Hayti recognized as an independent state.
		Gen. Hunter setting free slaves in the District of Columbia is checked; the Emancipation is reserved.
	May	All the Militia called out under arms. "The Capital is in danger."
		Lincoln's Day:—Rises early; two or three hours to private mail and news. 9 o'clock—breakfast; reads news and confers at War Office. *Home*—reads morning mail with secretary noting; answers some letters by hand. *Tuesday* and *Friday*—regular Cabinet councils; otherwise, visitors received by name, acquaintances preferred; three or four hours, "mostly office-seekers." 4 P.M., carriage drive with Mrs. Lincoln; 6 P.M. dinner, often with friends. 10 to midnight, "the rounds," public offices and military posts; finishing at the garrison general's for latest news.
	June	Confederate General J. E. B. Stuart's raid within Union lines.

1862		Continuous defeats of the Federal generals before Washington induce the President to confer with retired General Scott at West Point. On return, the President consolidated the Departments in Virginia under one head and placed over all General Pope, from the West, unjustified by his ranking position.
	July 2	Call for 300,000 three-years men.
	August	Answered Horace Greeley's open letter on slavery.
	Aug. 4	Call for 300,000 men, special, nine months.
	Sept. 8	General Lee enters Maryland.
	Sept. 22	Announcement that slavery will be abolished on the coming first of January.
	Nov. 5	General McClellan relieved by General Burnside.
	Dec. 8	"The Lincoln" Amnesty : Pardon to all laying down arms and swearing to defend the Constitution.
1863	Jan. 1	The Emancipation Proclamation. The Confederates given one hundred days to submit.
	Jan. 3	*Habeas Corpus* writ suspended and court-martial substituted for ordinary judicial proceedings.
	June 27	Confederates cross the Potomac and invade Pennsylvania.
	July 1–3	Battle of Gettysburg, Pa.; defeat of General Lee's Army.

1863	July 4	Vicksburg captured by General Grant.
		President's order : A Confederate prisoner to be put to hard labor for each colored Federal prisoner not treated as a prisoner of war.
	Sept. 13-16	"Draft" resistance riots in New York City.
	Sept. 17	Call for 300,000 three-years men.
		Speech at Philadelphia.
	Nov. 19	Speech at Gettysburg National Cemetery.
	Dec. 8	Proclamation of Amnesty and re-establishing certain States.
1864	Feb.	Call for 500,000 three-years men.
	Mar. 12	Ulysses S. Grant appointed Lieutenant-General and to command all the Federal armies.
	June 4	Fugitive Slave Law repealed.
	June 7	Abraham Lincoln renominated for President by Republican Convention, Baltimore.
	July 1	Secretary of Treasury Chase replaced by Fessenden, who holds office until March, 1865. "The Gold Bill" repealed: $1.00 gold worth $2.85 "greenback" note currency.
		Rich "bounties" offered substitutes for drafted men.
	July 12	Confederate General Early threatens Washington.

1864		Franco-Austrian Empire in Mexico.
		The President offers safe-conduct to volunteer peace negotiators, introduced by Horace Greeley.
	Oct. 19	Confederate raid from Canada into Vermont; a bank robbed.
	Dec. 6	President's Annual Message, reiteration; the Emancipation Act unaltered.
	Dec. 20	General Sherman at Savannah. "The backbone of the Rebellion broken."
1865	January	Exchange of prisoners.
	Mar. 4	Abraham Lincoln inaugurated, the second term.
	April 2	Richmond evacuated. Federals take possession and extinguish the set fires.
	April 9	General Lee capitulates.
	April 13	War Department Bulletin stays all military movements. On both sides, loss of men, 400,000. Cost $2,700,000,000.
	Apr. 14	The American flag restored upon Fort Sumter, by Major Anderson.
		The President assassinated by J. Wilkes Booth, at Washington; he died the next morning.
1865	April 19	Obsequies.

1865	April 21	Body lying in state ; taken to Springfield ; each city on the passage mourning.
	May 4	Burial at Springfield.
	May 24	President Andrew Johnson (the Vice-President of the second term) issues Amnesty Proclamation.
1866	Mar. 2	Peace proclaimed.
1867		Nebraska added to the Union.
1868	July 20	The XIVth Amendment proclaimed,
1874	Oct. 15	The Lincoln Monument dedicated.
1876	Nov. 7	Attempt to steal the body. Removed and deeply interred. To place Mrs. Lincoln's remains beside her husband's, both built in solidly.
1897		The Peterson House, where the President died, converted into the Lincoln Museum around the Oldroyd Lincoln collection, at Washington.
1898		"In Pulaski County, Ky., they are still voting for Abraham Lincoln, every Presidential election."—Louisville *Courier-Journal*, 1898.
1900	Mar. 10	Final deposit in the Monument, of Lincoln family remains, father, mother, sons, from Oak Ridge Cemetery.

Nil Magnum Nisi Bonum

LINCOLNICS

LINCOLNICS

"God Bless my Mother!"

"God bless my mother! all that I am, or hope to be, I owe to her!"

Lincoln lost his mother in 1818, when he was about eight years old. But she had taught him to read and write without books other than the Bible. Fortunately his father's second wife continued to nurture the boy on intellectual food and induced his father to send him to school. The general practice in the wilderness, where all were "short-handed," was to get the boys out a-field as much and as soon as possible.

You would Lose your Latin there.

Lincoln said of the rude frontier country where he was brought up: "If a straggler, supposed to understand Latin, happened to sojourn in the neighborhood, he was looked upon as a wizard." He knew no Latin except that found in his old copy of "Blackstone," and English law Latin—*Obscuris vera involvens!*

Lincoln's own Childish Horoscope.

(*Scribbled in a blank-book made by his hand.*)

"Abraham Lincoln
His hand and pen.
He will be good but
God knows when."

Juvenile Poetry.

(*Written* 1820, *but it may be a copy-book motto, then popular, and often set by the teacher.*)

"Good boys who to their books apply
Will all be great men by-and-by."

Respect for the Eggs, not the Hat.

In Lincoln's youth, when his attire was as unmodish as his appearance, he attended the performance of an itinerant juggler. The latter produced a bag of eggs and offered to make an omelet in a hat without injury to the latter. The trick, though dating back to the Dark Ages, was new to the spectators in the village, but the absence of hats prevented a ready tender of the required adjunct, until Abraham, urged forward by the neighbors, as wearing what might pass for a hat, handed up his headgear. It was woolly, of low-crowned and broad-brimmed shape, and had seen the worst sort of weather. In fact, the wearer apologized in these terms: "Mister, the reason why I did not offer you my hat before was out of respect for your eggs, not from care for the hat!"

After the Wrong Man.

At one time while Lincoln was engaged in chopping rails, the "bully of the county" (Sangamon, Ill.), perhaps set on by some practical joker, came to "the boys" in the woods and, with set design, challenged "the greeny" (Lincoln) to a fight.

The great brawny, awkward boy laughed and drawled out: "I reckon, stranger, you 're after the wrong man. I never *fit* in my whole life." But the bully made for Abe, and in the first fall Lincoln came down on top of the heap. The champion was bruising and causing blood to flow down Lincoln's face, when a happy mode of warfare entered his original brain. He quickly thrust his hands into a convenient bunch of smartweed and rubbed the same in the eyes of his opponent, who almost instantly begged for mercy. He was released, but his sight, for the time being, was extinct. No member of the trio possessed a pocket handkerchief, so Lincoln tore from his own shirt front the surplus cloth, washed and bandaged the fellow's eyes and sent him home.

John White, reprinted in Viroqua, Wis., *Censor*.

Making the Wool Fly.

On Lincoln's first trip to New Orleans on a flatboat, he, and his crew of one, were attacked by negroes at Baton Rouge. In a brisk hand-to-hand resistance, the thieves were repelled. After their flight Abraham's companion regretted that they had not carried guns.

"If armed, would n't we have made the feathers fly?" said he.

"The *wool,* you mean!" corrected the other, "as they were not that kind of *black birds*."

If You Hit, Hit Hard!

On coming out of a slave auction salesroom in New Orleans, Lincoln, who had conducted a freighted flatboat down the Mississippi from Indiana, remarked to his crew:

"If ever I get a chance to hit that thing [slavery], I 'll hit it hard."

In a Whipping, the Whip-Hand Matters not.

When Lincoln was 'prentice to the grocery business, at Thomas Affut's (Offutt?) store, 1831, a customer used language inadmissible in the presence of "ladies." The young man remonstrated with the offender, but made voluble by the potations he had imbibed (for the grocery on the border was a drinking saloon as well), he persisted in his "cuss" words. When this language had driven out the ladies, the clerk was entertained with the same Billingsgate, upon which, getting his word in at a pause for breath, he said:

"As you are set on getting a whipping, *I* may as well give it to you as any other man"; thereupon he flung the customer out-of-doors (he is reported as having on a public occasion "thrown a man ten or twelve feet"), and following him up, gave him a thrashing. As the delinquent would not cry "quarter!" he rubbed smartweed in his eyes till he "caved in." This smartweed seems in frontier warfare to have taken the place of that dagger-of-mercy with which an obdurate knight was tickled when he would not sue for grace. It was made use of in another pugilistic exploit of our hero.

The Long and the Short.

When Lincoln was "keeping store," one of the gossiping frequenters of the place was a "Captain" Larkins, a great boaster. He was as short and stout as the young storekeeper was tall and lean. One day he was declaring that he had the best and fastest horse in town. "I ran him three mile' in nine minutes, and he never fetched a long breath."

Lincoln looked down over the bar on the little braggart, and asked:

"But, Larkins, why do you not tell us how many *short* breaths he drew?"

A New Military Command.

When Lincoln was Captain of the "Bucktail" Rangers in the Black Hawk War, 1832, he was as ignorant of military matters as his company was of drill or of tactics. The test came when his troop, formed by platoons, confronted a gate. The Captain had no idea of the proper order; but his wit did not desert him. He ordered:

"This company is dismissed for two minutes, when it will fall in, *on the other side of that fence!*" (He characterized this as "an endwise" movement.)

Even in after years when the Lawgiver had to be also Commander-in-Chief, he did not pretend to any military knowledge.

Let them Laugh, if it Works well.

There is preserved in the Patent Office, at Washington, unless it has been removed to the National Lincoln Museum, a model, whittled out of wood, for a device to enable a flatboat to overcome various riparian obstacles. It is of Abraham Lincoln's invention. It was a device of the days when he was a legislator and legal practitioner. But before that, his original turn of mind had led him in that same direction. While navigating a flatboat of his own building, in 1831, on a salt creek—not the Salt River of political renown—Lincoln fitted the craft with sails made of boards and canvas, which succeeded fairly well in saving the hard work of poling, but which excited the merriment of the beholders. At Beardstown, the inhabitants turned out to line the bank and laugh at the apparition. Lincoln's companions were annoyed, but he said:

"Let them laugh, so long as the thing works well."

"An Old Woman's Dance—Short and Sweet."[1]

"My politics are short and sweet, like an old woman's dance."

Maiden Speech, Pappsville or Richland, Ill., 1832.

No Ambition so Great as True Esteem.

"Every man is said to have his peculiar ambition. Whether that be true or not, I can say, for one, that I have no other so great as that of being truly esteemed of my fellow-men, by rendering myself worthy of their esteem."

Speech, 1832.

"If Elected, Thankful; if not, All the Same."

The first of the Lincoln speeches in active politics runs thus:

---

[1] The Old World proverb is: "Short and sweet: a donkey's gallop."

"Gentlemen and Fellow-citizens: I presume you all know who I am. I am humble Abraham Lincoln. . . . My politics are short and sweet, etc. . . . I am in favor of the internal improvement system and a high protective tariff. . . . If elected, I shall be thankful; if not, it will be all the same."

1832.

"Better Sometimes Right than at All Times Wrong."

"I hold it a sound maxim that it is better only sometimes to be right, than at all times to be wrong."

Speech as candidate for the Illinois Legislature, March, 1832.

Action Speaks Louder than Words.

Lincoln's first speech in behalf of his endeavor to enter the Legislature in 1832 was made in the summer, after an auction sale at Pappsville, Ill. Interrupted by a fight in the audience and seeing that one of his supporters was being "whipped" he leaped off the improvised rostrum and seizing the victor flung him "ten or twelve feet" from his prey. He then returned to finish his harangue amid such applause as would in the "wild West" always greet a manifestation of physical prowess.[1] Hence when the polling came, such a master of fisticuffs secured the hearty support of the voters.

The Best Way to Efface Unpleasantness.

"Meet face to face and converse together—the best way to efface unpleasant feeling."

Letter to Judge Berdan, of Jacksonville, Ill., during the Lincoln campaign for the Legislature.

---

[1] The people there and then were of the mind of the boy in *Punch*, who, replying to the maternal reproach that he was behind another in education, said: "I cannot talk French like him, but I can punch his head!"

"A Mighty Handy Little Fellow."

Lincoln is recorded as having said of the semicolon, that it was "a mighty handy little fellow."

"I Want To—The Worst Way."

Lincoln's first love romance occurred in 1833. He was captivated by the village belle of New Salem, Ill. She was a Miss Anne Rutledge, whose father kept the tavern. In another two years, they were engaged but she died a few months later. The effect on the suitor was profound and appears to have continued through life.[1] But, in 1839, while his friends were seeking distractions for him, and while he was engaged in the practice of law in Springfield, he met there a Miss Mary Todd. She came from his own native State, Kentucky. It is of note that

[1] Those cruel romance-breakers, the physicians, however, ascribe the President's settled melancholy to confirmed dyspepsia, due to the insufficient and irregular nutrition of his childhood and of the early days of pecuniary want.

his rival in this suit was Stephen A. Douglas, afterwards his opponent in the political arena. Miss Todd made the disconsolate one a happy man on the fourth of November, 1842. The wedding day had first been set for January, 1841, but Lincoln seemed to regard it as "a fatal day" and it was postponed. Whatever the cause of the delay, friends saw that the swain's melancholy required some such remedy as was to be secured through the vivacity and attractiveness of the fair Kentuckian, and all were in a harmless conspiracy to bring about the match.

One evening, at a party,[1] Lincoln approached Miss Todd, seated among the wall-flowers, and timidly asked in his vernacular, which still clung to him and which he retained for effective expression through life:

"I should like to dance with you *the worst way!*"

---

[1] Related by General Singleton, of Quincy, Illinois, a brother lawyer.

The invitation was accepted, and the victim dragged her unlicked bear cub around with her in the whirls of the waltz; the steps which might have won claps and whoops of applause on the cabin floor or the flatboat deck not being recognized as *à la mode* in Springfield When the lady was restored to her companions, one quizzically inquired:

"Well, Mary, did not Mr. Lincoln dance with you 'the worst way'?"

"The very worst," was her reply.

It must be credited to her that she was almost the only person, at that early stage, to foresee supremacy in the uncouth man and to assert that he would one day attain to high station.

A Lightning-Rod for a Guilty Conscience.

In the campaign of 1836 Lincoln was attacked at Springfield by an old citizen, one Forquer, who had quitted the Whigs and had been appointed Land Office registrar as if in recognition of his apostacy.

Mr. Forquer had just completed a new house and had placed on it what was then a great novelty—a lightning-rod. In his speech, Forquer undertook "to take the young man down." The young aspirant arose and replied as follows:

"Mr. Forquer commenced his speech by announcing that 'the young man was to be taken down.' It is for you, fellow-citizens, not me, to say whether I am up or down. . . . . I desire to live, and I desire place and distinction, but I would rather die now than, like this gentleman, live to see the day when I would change my politics for an office worth three thousand dollars a year, and then feel obliged to erect a lightning-rod over my house to protect a guilty conscience from an offended God!"

The Rough Diamond Cuts the Polished One.

As has been frequently noted, men without personal attractions, like Mirabeau, George Wilkes, and others, have succeeded in winning their way by cultivating the purely conversational or oratorical graces. This is of great advantage in those electioneering campaigns where the voters are canvassed man by man. In one of these conflicts Lincoln and his Democratic opponent, L. D. Ewing, contended in company for the ballot of a prominent farmer in Sangamon County. He was not at home when they called so the two set to work with the "gray mare." But neither made much progress till milking time when they both started out with her to help with the pail and stool. Arrived at the barn door, Mr. Ewing took the pail and insisted on doing the milking himself. While stroking the cow he naturally concluded he was making the master-stroke—for the vote. But as he received no reply to the bits of speech delivered at intervals, he looked up finally only to see the hostess and his rival leaning on the bars at ease, in amicable discussion. By the time his task was done, Lincoln had captivated the voter's better half and all that the other gleaned for his kindness was hearty thanks for giving her a chance "to have *so* pleasant a talk with Mr. Lincoln!"

Told by Judge L. D. Ewing, Chicago.

Make the World Better for Your Having Lived in it.

On account of the breaking of his marriage engagement, Lincoln fell into a state of gloom that was alarming to his friends, who assured him that he must rally or lose his life. He failed to attend the Legislature, of which he was member (1841), and neglected his private duties. On recovering, he said to his friend, Mr. Speed:

"I have an inexpressible desire to live till I can be assured that the world is a little better for my having lived in it."

A Narrow Squeak for the Pig.

During Lincoln's early days when he was poor and depressed by the profound despondency which so long afflicted him, he was riding one day through the sparsely settled parts of Indiana. His errand was of importance, and he was dressed in his best—home-spun jeans. But he gave ear to a shrill cry of distress at which his companions only laughed. It was but a pig caught in the mud of a wallow, and sinking so fast that it would shortly cut its throat with its sharp feet or suffocate. Lincoln looked at the black *gumbo* mud, then at his good clothes, "the unique Sunday-go-to-meetings," and after a slight hesitation, turned back and extricated the little porker. When he went onwards, he was daubed with mud. But he explained to his friends that he thought of the poor farmer who could not afford such a loss and he thought also of the shote and could not resist the appeal.

The Prize for Homeliness.

Abraham Lincoln did not deceive himself in regard to his facial blemishes. George Sand has said that every man is pleased with his face but never with his fortune. The President gives the lady the lie on that axiom. It may be premised that, on the border, a person remarkably ill-favored in lineaments was awarded a jack-knife as token of his preëminence in this line.

Lincoln tells the story of how he became possessed of this undesirable trophy.

"In the days when I used to be on the circuit [183-, travelling on horseback from one county court to another] I was once accosted by a stranger, who said:

"'Excuse me, sir, but I have an article which belongs to you.'

"'How is that?' I asked, considerably astonished.

"The stranger took a jack-knife from his pocket.

"'This knife,' said he, 'was placed in my hands some years ago, with the injunction that I was to keep it until I found a man homelier-looking than I am myself. I have carried it from that time till this; allow me to say, sir, that you are fairly entitled to the property.'"

As "below the lowest depth" there is a lower still, Lincoln was also able to make a happy deliverance of the token to another victim of fate. But the latter, the Rev. William Hastings, rejoicing at its being the link which connected him with the President of the United States, proclaimed the fact at Toronto, Canada, where he lived and died (Feb., 1902), a revered minister of the Gospel.

"Not One of the Sparrows is Forgotten."

Another time when Lincoln was riding over the prairie with a party of law-court attendants, they noticed a couple of fledglings fluttering on the ground where they had fallen out of the nest. After the party had gone on a little distance, Lincoln wheeled and rode back on their tracks. The others halted and watched him go to the spot and replace the nestlings.

When he rejoined the cavalcade, one of the men bantered him about his charitable act, saying:

"Why did you bother yourself and delay us about such a trifle?"

"My friend," was the response, "I can only say that I feel the better for it!"

As there were several witnesses of this incident, accounts vary as to the number of birdlings, but, as usual, this variant proves the fact.

Turn About Is Fair Play.

"My only argument (in politics) is that 'turn about is fair play'" (in regard to a candidate giving way to another candidate for the party good—with the understanding that the relinquishing one represents the party in the next election).

As a matter of fact, the opponent withdrew.

[*Letter* held by Dr. Boal, Lacon, Ill.]

A Venture on Nothing.

As a boy, Lincoln had often attracted attention and commendation by giving his spare time to reading. One inquirer as to the nature of his studies was surprised that he should answer "Law." It was the bending of the twig which inclined the tree. He had picked up a copy of "Blackstone" from the rubbish in the barrel of a second-hand clothes-and-odds dealer travelling through the country. With scarcely more than this provision, and what he had gleaned from odd volumes of the State Statutes, in 1837, at the age of twenty-eight, he arrived in

Springfield to engage definitely in the practice of law. He rode on a hired horse and his property was contained in a pair of saddle-bags. He priced at the town stores the outfit for a single bed. It came to seventeen dollars, more than he could pay, but he proposed to Joshua F. Speed, the storekeeper, to buy the bed subject to payment at Christmas, by which time he hoped his law undertakings would be fruitful. The merchant naturally objected that he might fail.

"If I fail in this," was the sad reply, "I will probably never be able to pay you."

The storekeeper kindly suggested that he should "room" with him as he had a double-bedded room; and a friend allowed him board "till his ship came in." The great problem of bed and board was thus solved for the aspirant. This action was what was called "neighborly" in those parts and in those days; and without giving grounds for Lincoln's refusing ees from needy clients, it prompted him o do unto others as he had been done by.

"A Land of Free Speech."

When Lincoln was in partnership with ohn T. Stuart, they had offices directly ver the courtroom in Springfield. This llowed them to overhear the proceedings elow them, much after the mode in which)'Artagnan, in the *Musketeers,* listened t the trap-hole in his floor to what went n beneath it. There was, indeed, a novable board, and at the aperture, re-lining at full length, Lincoln would take iote of the progress of a case until the it moment for his attendance.

During a holiday of the bench, a crowd illed the courtroom and a friend of Lin-oln, Edward D. Baker, was addressing hem, when something adverse in his iarangue incited the unruly to assault he speaker and to pull him down. By a iappy chance, Lincoln was lending his ear to the discussion, and, peering down through the hole in the floor, perceived the danger of his friend. Immediately, without delaying to run around and descend by the stairs, he thrust his big feet and long legs through the opening and dropped like a bolt out of the sky into the *mêlée.*

Picking up a water-jug, and striking an attitude of defence, he shouted:

"Hold on, gentlemen, this is a land of free speech! Mr. Baker has a right to be heard. I am here to protect him, and no man shall take him from this stand if I can prevent it."

This dictum of the *Deus ex machina* imposed order and the orator was allowed to continue his speech.

The Voice out of Proportion to the Body.

Once during the argument in a lawsuit, in which Lincoln represented one party, the lawyer on the other side was a good deal of a talker, but was not reckoned as deeply profound or much of a thinker. He would say anything to a jury which happened to enter his head. Lincoln, in his address to the jury, referring to this, said:

"My friend on the other side is all right, or would be all right, were it not for the peculiarity I am about to chronicle. His habit—of which you have witnessed a very painful specimen in his argument to you in this case—of reckless assertion and statements without grounds, need not be imputed to him as a moral fault or as telling of a moral blemish. He can't help it. For reasons which, gentlemen of the jury, you and I have not the time to study here, as deplorable as they are surprising, the oratory of the gentleman completely suspends all action of his mind. The moment he begins to talk, his mental operations cease. I never knew of but one thing which compared with my friend in this particular. That was a small steamboat. Back in the days when I performed my part as a keel boatman [1830], I made the acquaintance of a trifling little steamboat which used to bustle and puff and wheeze about the Sangamon River. It had a five-foot boiler and a seven-foot whistle, and every time it whistled it stopped."

[*Argonaut.*]

"Settle It!"

Squire Masters of Petersburg, Ill., was once threatened with a lawsuit. He went to Springfield, where Lincoln was located [1837, etc.], and had a talk with him about the case. Lincoln told him, as an old friend, that if he could not settle the case he would undertake the defence but he urged his friend to make an amicable adjustment.

"What 'll you charge, Abe, to go into court for me?" said Mr. Masters.

"Well," was Lincoln's reply, "it wil

cost you ten dollars; but I won't charge you anything if you can settle it between yourselves."

The other party heard of the squire's visit to Lincoln, and agreed to settle.

A Lawyer with a Conscience.

A lawyer who studied in Mr. Lincoln's office tells a story illustrative of his love of justice. After listening one day for some time to a client's statement of his case, Lincoln, who had been staring at the ceiling, suddenly swung around in his chair, and said:

"Well, you have a pretty good case in technical law, but a pretty bad one in equity and justice. You'll have to get some other fellow to win this case for you. I could n't do it. All the time, while talking to that jury, I'd be thinking: 'Lincoln, you're a liar,' and I believe I should forget myself and say it out loud."

Tit for Tat.

During the forties, when Lincoln was living in Springfield, practising law, there was among his patrons a judge, an influential citizen, of whose dignity more care was taken by his associates than by himself. On his part, the budding barrister (to use the English term) was still not over-particular as to appearance or attire; he would have agreed with Dr. Johnson who boldly averred that he had "no passion for fine linen." In his attitudes, also, he was, to put it mildly, careless. When the judge was ushered into the parlor he was, therefore, not astonished to see the long, attenuated figure spread over at least two chairs, reclining rather than sitting, quite at his ease. It is noticeable in those who have been brought up to hard work that they are apt to procure entire rest by lying prone; the boy Lincoln was often seen reading or writing on the earth floor or on the unswept hearthstone. He did not change his position after the caller was seated, somewhat more decorously. Mrs. Lincoln, from the reply to her chance question put to the servant, suspected something of the matter. She hurried into the presence of the two lawyers and found herself so shocked at the unseemly demeanor of her husband that she went up behind the sinner, plucked him by the hair (worn long in the far-Western style), and twitched his head up and around with a reminding look.

The sufferer apparently did not notice the double rebuke; he simply looked at her and said, without changing a muscle:

"*Little Mary!* allow me to introduce you to my friend, Judge Butterfield!"

Now it is well known that nothing is more deeply felt or more warmly resented by undersized persons than any allusion to their stature. Lincoln habitually alluded to his partner as "the little woman." And, unfortunately, the discrepancy between Mrs. Lincoln and her giant mate was of frequent remark and of continual consciousness, so that she came out of this encounter the humiliated one. The judge might conclude that this instance impugned the ancient saying that the " Eagle in the rostrum is a dove at home."

Not Fate but Providence.

" What is to be, will be!—or, rather, I have found out, all my life, as Hamlet says: 'There 's a divinity that shapes our ends, rough-hew them how we will.' "

[*Letter* to Mr. John Butterfield, of Chicago, 1841.]

This line from *Hamlet* would appeal to one who had exercised the woodman's art. With the felling axe, one rough-hews the log, but it is a superior hand that shapes all to the finish.

In connection with this expression of belief in predestination, it may be related that once during a conversation with Senator Dawes (Mass.) the President took up the Senator's little boy in his arms and said to him, with humorous gravity:

"My boy, never *try* to be President! If you do, you never will be."

This classes the President apart from the denier of the predestinarian doctrine who said in reply to an argument: "No! I believe that what will be, won't be!"

Lincoln's Favorite Shakespeare Play.

Macbeth. The coincidence of the regicide has frequently been noted.

Lincoln on Shakespeare.

"The best judge of human nature that ever wrote."

"Slow to Learn and Slow to Forget."

An intimate friend of Lincoln, Mr. J. F. Speed, of Springfield, had remarked that Lincoln's mind was a wonder to him, as impressions seemed easily made upon it and were never effaced.

"No," corrected Lincoln, "you are mistaken. I am slow to learn and slow to forget that which I have learned. My mind is like a piece of steel—very hard to scratch anything upon it, and almost impossible, after you get it there, to rub it out."

The Chief Gem of Character is to Keep One's Resolves.

"Before I resolve to do the one thing or the other, I must gain my confidence in my own ability to keep my resolves when they are made."

[*Letter* to J. F. Speed, July, 1842.]

"Hug a Bad Bargain all the Tighter."

In another letter to Mr. Speed, Lincoln says that his father had a saying:

"If you make a bad bargain, hug it all the tighter!"

[Feb., 1842.]

Representing by Proxy.

The Whig primary convention held at Springfield, Ill., in 1842, chose, as candidates, Abraham Lincoln, Edward D. Baker and John J. Hardin. The last was the favorite and Lincoln had "a tax of considerable per cent. levied on his strength," as this man was to be elected. As it happened that Baker had the next term, and Lincoln the one following, in 1846, a cry of collusion was not unnaturally raised, but this is said to have been *illusion.* When the selection was decided by acclamation, Lincoln proposed that Baker should have the following term, but his generosity was received by a majority of but one vote. Lincoln said he felt like the young man who had been "cut out" but who was consolingly invited, when the other fellow married his "girl," to act as "best man."

Historical Note.—Of these three rivals and finally successful candidates, all met violent deaths: Hardin was killed at the battle of Buena Vista, in the Mexican War, and Baker at Ball's Bluff, in the Civil War.

Do not Wait to be Hunted Up and Pushed Forward.

"Do you suppose that I should ever have got into notice if I had waited to be hunted up and pushed forward by older men?"

[*Letter* to Judge Herndon, 1848.]

A Small Crop of Fight from a Big Piece of Ground.

In a case of assault and battery, Lincoln was assigned to the defence. The plaintiff made out a strong story of the injuries done him, which his appearance bore out. Having finished exhibiting his maltreated client, the district attorney handed him over to the defence for cross-examination. Lincoln had studied the plaintiff rather than his evidence, and reasoned that he must break down the complaint or discredit the accusation. He conceived that the fellow was a conceited one who would by replying saucily seek to show himself "smart."

"Well, my friend," demanded he, suddenly, after a pause to "reckon him up," "how much ground did you and my client here fight over?"

"About six acres," answered the man, pertly.

"Well, but do you not allow that was a mighty small crop of a fight to gather off such a big piece of ground?"

The result was a laugh which ended in "laughing the matter out of court."

Told by Hon. Chauncey Depew, in Rice's *Recollections*.

Litigation.

"Discourage litigation! There will still be business enough."

Notes for a Lecture on the Law.

Extempore Speaking.

" Extempore speaking is the lawyer's avenue to the people."

Notes for a Lecture on the Law.

Diligence.

" The leading rule for the lawyer, as for the man of any other calling, is Diligence."

Notes for a Lecture on the Law.

" Come and Help me Let Go ! "

The law firm of Herndon and Lincoln [1843, etc.] had the defence in a capital case in which the judge had shown himself adverse to them and to their client. Lincoln, who was the voice of his side, felt that the rulings were personal and said in the recess:

" I have determined to 'crowd the court to the wall,' and to regain my position before night." " Mad all over," he upbraided the bench, within due bounds, and at the end had "peeled the court from head to foot," figuratively declares his law partner. To clinch the argument, says the same reporter, he made use of a locally applicable simile.

"In early days," said Lincoln, "a party of men went out hunting for a wild boar. But the game came upon them unawares, and they, scampering away, climbed trees, all save one, who, seizing the animal by the ears, undertook to hold him. After holding him for some time and finding his strength giving way, he cried out to his companions in the trees:

"'Boys, come down and help me let go!'"

The scarified judge pretended to see his error and reversed his decision, and Lincoln's client was acquitted.

Judge Herndon's *Life*.

Suspicion and Jealousy.

"Suspicion and jealousy never did help any man in any situation."

Letter to Judge Herndon, July, 1848.

Don't Contest a Clear Right.

On inspecting the evidence exhibited to Lincoln by a lawyer bringing suit to enforce the specific execution of a contract, the advocate said:

"As your client is justly entitled to a decree in his favor, I shall so represent it to the court. It is against my principles to contest a clear matter of right."

Legal Rights Are not always Moral Rights.

A would-be client detailed to Lincoln, at Springfield, Ill., a case in which he had a legal claim to a value of some hundreds of dollars. But his winning it would ruin a widow and afflict her six children.

"We shall not take your case, though we can doubtless gain it for you," responded Lincoln. "Some things that are right legally are not right morally.

But we will give you some advice for which we will charge nothing. [The "we" included his partner, Mr. Herndon.] We advise a sprightly, energetic man like you to try your hand at making six hundred dollars in some other way."

Coming into Court with Clean Hands.

While Lincoln was a practising lawyer, he had lost a case from the defendant's producing a receipt for the sum in question. Lincoln immediately retired. The court sent for him, and the messenger found him in the neighborhood hotel washing his hands.

"My hands are dirty from that 'slippery knave,'" said he, and, using the towel, "I want to return to court with clean hands."

The Presidency Was so Big.

Lincoln's first ambition—when "clerking it" in a country store—was to be member of the State Assembly. Later he longed to be Congressman. Then—at the time when the railroad magnate Villard, made his acquaintance out West—he said: "I did not consider myself quali fied for the U. S. Senatorship and i took me a long time to persuade mysel that I was." He became convinced o that later, but still he kept on saying t himself: "'It is too big a thing fo you, Abe; you will never get it!' Mar [Mrs. Lincoln] insists that I am going t be Senator and President of the Unite States!" This was followed, continue the narrator, by a roar of laughter, as h sat with his arms around his knees, shak ing all over with mirth at his wife's am bition. "Just think," he exclaimed, "o such a *sucker*[1] as me for President!"

---

[1] Sucker in this sense means a native o citizen of Illinois, the "Sucker State." Th marshy nature of the land near the first settle ments by the rich river bottom, full o mud-fish of the lamprey order, and thei manner of feeding suggested the nickname

"Keep the Pledge!"

In the forties, the "teetotal" or tem-
erance movement, originating in Great
Britain, swept through the States even to
he borders. At the front was an or-
anization called the "Washingtonians."
t had been instituted at Washington, on
he 22d of February, 1842. About
846, Illinois experienced the agitation,
kin to a religious revival. Abraham
incoln was the lecturer to the society, in
he South Fork schoolhouse, Sangamon
ounty. He had, in his general-store ex-
erience, seen the evils of the drink habit
nd the system fostering it. Among the

---

ogether with the coincidence that, as the
suckers" ascend the stream and return at
ertain seasons, the natives of "Egypt," around
airo, went up to work at times in the Galena
ad mines but came home to till their farms.
(Compare with General Washington's reply to
ongress on being appointed Commander-in-
hief: "I declare with the utmost sincerity,
do not think myself equal to the commission
am honored with."—June, 1776.)

youth who assumed the blue ribbon an(took the pledge was one Cleophas Breckenridge, to whom the orator said, on decorating him:

"Now, sonny, you keep that pledg(and it will be the best act of your life!'

Never Drink—Never a Drunkard.

Lincoln used to repeat a remark of hi stepmother's in reference to his early adoption and advocacy of the temperanc(movement:

"Men become drunkards because the; begin to drink; if they never begai to drink they would never becom(drunkards."

If Any Man Thinks it Easy to b(President, let him Try it!

There is an ancient saying, coeval witl the Greeks, that the pleasure is in th(race, not in the palm, its prize. Lincoli proved the truth of this as early as hi election as Congressman and consequen arrival at the Mecca of all successful politicians, Washington. He wrote to an intimate correspondent, in 1846, when his foot was at the ball, " Being elected . . . . has not pleased me as much as I expected." His friends were sure that he would distinguish himself there, but it was much more like an extinguishment; he, the man of the people from the start, actually ran counter to popularity by opposing the general desire for war with Mexico, at the bottom of which question lay the tremendous doctrine of " Free soil for free settlers." Under all the arguments, however, was the hunger for land—land! and Texas had long been doomed to be clutched by the Northern eagle's claw. But, immediately after the war, and while the aroma of victory still clung to him, old " Rough and Ready " —surely a hero after his own kind—was nominated for President [1848], and Lincoln somewhat illogically stood up for Zachary Taylor. He made speeches on his behalf in Massachusetts. He pleaded that the General, while the figurehead of the Whig party, held correct sound "Republican" principles.[1] This double-header was naturally applauded by numbers of Messrs. Facing-both-ways. The result was that Gen. Zachary Taylor was our twelfth President.

When Lincoln became the sixteenth, he learned thoroughly of "polished perturbation." Nine tenths of his callers were office-seekers for self or kin, or supplicants for contracts; his house was divided, as his wife's connections at least sympathized with the wrong side; and his responsibility weighed heavily upon him as he had no second—no other-self—no Mazarin, at the worst, with whom to share it.

---

[1] The Republican party as a concrete organization did not come into existence till 1856 when it was built on the "free soil" ("squatter sovereignty") question.

Too Slow for a Hearse!

A portrait of Lincoln, seen in a St. Louis art exhibition, was the work of A. J. Conant, who, to keep his sitter in good countenance, used to "swap stories" with him. One of Lincoln's runs as follows:

"There was a man from Missouri who went to a 'livery' to get a horse to take him to a convention, where he expected to be made a delegate. The stable-keeper was of another political stripe, and naturally fobbed off upon him a horse calculated to break down before he reached his destination. On his return home, the disappointed Missourian asked the proprietor if he was training that animal to draw a hearse.

"'Guess I ain't' was the surly reply.

"'Well,' went on the other, "'if you were, he would never do for it; for he would not get the corpse to the cemetery in time for the resurrection.'"

The eminent story-teller was fond of this story—so the relater proceeds,—as he had twice been interrupted in the delivery of it; once by a railroad train "pulling out" as he began it, and again, at a great gun testing, by the ordnance going off just at the point of the narrative.

He Wanted the Pork!

At a meeting during an electioneering campaign, one of the audience asked Lincoln a question which he did not answer. This seemed singular as, usually, he was glad to reply and to show his readiness and ability to turn the tables when being "heckled." A supporter on the platform inquired the reason of his taciturnity. "I am after votes," whispered Lincoln with his ironical wink and working his lips like a horse when trying to get the bit between his teeth, "and that man's vote is as good as any other man's!"

"The Common-[Looking] People."

Lincoln once dreamed that he was in a great assembly where the people made a lane for him to pass through. "He is a common-looking fellow," said one of them. "Friend," replied Lincoln in his dream, "the Lord prefers common-looking people—that is why He made so many of them."

Hapgood's *Abraham Lincoln.*

The current quotation reads: "The Lord loves the poor more than the rich, because He (or He would not have) made so many of them."

Lincoln's Early Library.

The Bible, Dilworth's *Spelling-book,* Kirkham's *Grammar,* Euclid, Shakespeare, Volney's *Ruins,* Paine's *Age of Reason,* Blackstone, Illinois State Statutes, Burns, Æsop's *Fables, Life of Franklin, Pilgrim's Progress,* Weems's *Washington* and Ramsay's, Riley's *Nar-*

rative, Holmes's *Poems,* Chas. Mackay's *Poems,* Cowper's *Poems.*

Protection to Make a Great Country.

"My fellow-citizens, I may not live to see it, but give us a protective tariff, and we will have the greatest country on earth."

Reported by Mr. R. Grigsby, *Speech* in Indiana, 1844.

Books Show our Thoughts are not New.

An Illinois minister having observed to Congressman Lincoln that "Men of force can get on without books—they do their own thinking," the other replied: "Yes; but books serve to show that those original thoughts of his are n't very new."

Taking More than My Share.

When Congressman Lincoln paid his first visit in that capacity to the national capital, he had had no acquaintance with what was, in the North and East, esteemed "good society." In the House lobby and its sanctum for airing witticisms, as well as in his boarding-house coffee-room, he speedily became the pre-eminent conversationalist; but it could hardly be expected that the "Hoosier" would adorn the drawing-room of the "first families." He seems to have been lured into these uncongenial haunts much as Voltaire's "Huron" was led through the salons of King Louis, although his shrewd innate sense and honest simplicity saved him from embarrassment no less creditably than was the case with Franklin, when the duchesses "smoked" him at his retreat in Passy.

It is recounted that, at a dinner, where the joint was the not uncommon leg of roast mutton, the inevitable currant jelly accompanying it was passed in its own glass. But the guest, in perfect innocence, took the latter and clung to it, eating of it steadily. The butler knew his business, however, and, as in the epicurean anecdote of the Two Salmons, simply sent a second glass of jelly on its rounds. It was still circulating when the offender, perceiving that something was wrong, laughed quietly at seeing that his neighbors took only a spoonful from the glass, and observed *not* inaudibly:

"It seems that I took more than my share!" He went on with the repast, the whole blunder and honest retrievement being accepted as proving good manners at heart.

No Military Hero.

Although a member of Lincoln's Cabinet said that "The President is his own war minister; he directs personally the movements of the armies and is fond of strategy," yet he relieved himself of the superior command with the utmost readiness when the able Atlas appeared in General Grant. At all events, in earlier years Lincoln treated humorously his martial experience during the "Black Hawk War." The Democratic candidate for President, when Lincoln was in Congress [1846], was General Cass, for whom political capital was attempted to be made of his conduct in that war. Lincoln descanted upon this claim as follows:

"Mr. Speaker, did you know that *I* am a military hero? Yes, sir, in the days of the Black Hawk War I fought, bled and—came away. Speaking of General Cass's career reminds me of my own. I was not at Stillman's defeat; but I was about as near it as Cass was to Hull's surrender, and like him I saw the place very soon afterward. It is quite certain I did not break my sword, for I had none to break,[1] but I bent my musket pretty badly. . . . If Gen. Cass went in advance of me in picking whortle-berries, I guess I surpassed him in charges upon the wild

[1] Although captain of rangers at the outset, Lincoln enlisted as a private of volunteers on the second call.

onions. If he saw any live fighting Indians [1] it was more than I did, but I had a good many bloody struggles with the mosquitoes; and, although I never fainted from the loss of blood, I can truly say I was often very hungry. . . . If I should ever turn Democrat and be taken up as a candidate by the Democratic party, I protest they shall not make fun of me as they have of General Cass by attempting to make me out *a military hero*."

Between the Saddle and the Ground.

It was providential that the Western statesman should have his vision widened. One may see the hand of Heaven, not the finger of Fate, beckoning him to that eventful tour in Massachusetts, in 1848, in which he met a powerful suggestion

[1] The only Indian Lincoln's company captured was a civilized one, whom he saved from maltreatment.

for the great act of his life, the freeing of the Southern slaves. In Tremont Temple, Boston, in September, he listened to the ringing speech of William H. Seward; and was prompted to say to the orator, that night:

"Governor, I have been thinking about what you said. I reckon you are right! We *have* got to deal with this slavery question."

The sincerity of his conversion to the extreme doctrine may be inferred from his selection of Seward for his Secretary of State, an honor that nearly cost Seward his life. Time came when the pupil and the leader were to move side by side, with the latter using the old war-cry: "All men, of any color, free!"

"Unite—And the Race is Ours."

"If all those who wish to keep up the character of the Union, who do not believe in enlarging our field, but in keeping our fences where they are, and cultivating our present possessions, making it a garden, improving the morals and education of the people, devoting the administrations to this purpose—all real Whigs, friends of good honest government—will unite, the race is ours."

Speech at Worcester, Mass., 1848.

Judging the Consequences Points out our Duty.

"When divine or human law does not clearly point out what is our duty, we have no means of finding out what it is but using our most intelligent judgment of the consequences."

Speech at Worcester, Mass., 1848.

"Pantaloons Large Enough for any Man—Small Enough for any Boy."

"If the 'Free Soil' platform held any other principle than opposition to the extension of slavery in new territory, it

was in such a general way that it was like the pair of pantaloons the Yankee pedler offered for sale, 'Large enough for any man—small enough for any boy.'"
Speech at Worcester, Mass., Sept., 1848.

If Youth Would and Age Could.

When Abraham Lincoln applied in 1848 to President Taylor, in whose election he had vigorously assisted, for the commissionership of the Land Office, he was offered instead the governorship of Oregon Territory. The other place had been assigned to Mr. Justin Butterfield of Chicago. During the war, when the son of the successful office-seeker requested a military commission of Lincoln, now President, the latter, at the name, recurred to his rebuff and remarked:

"I have hardly ever felt so bad at any failure, and I have often been sorry that I did not accept the governorship of Oregon."

"How fortunate that you declined, sir," responded the young man: "You might have come back as Senator [this was a sort of "rider" to the berth], but you would never have been President."

"You are probably right," returned the President, reflecting.

Elevate Men, Do Not Debase Them.

"As I understand the spirit of our institutions, it is designed to promote the elevation of men. I am therefore hostile to anything that tends to their debasement."

To Rise, Improve Yourself.

"The way for a young man to rise is to improve himself every way he can, never suspecting that anybody wishes to hinder him."

Letter to Judge Herndon, July, 1848.

Stand with the Right!

"Stand with anybody that stands right. Stand with him while he is right and part with him when he goes wrong."

"Let none Falter Who Thinks He is Right."

Military Glory.

"Military glory—that attractive rainbow that rises in showers of blood; that serpent's eye that charms to destroy!"

"The Monarch of All He Surveyed."

In the middle of the last century, E. F. Beale, afterwards General, was Surveyor-general to California, where he surveyed—that is, *conveyed*—a large tract of land to his own estate, and the fact was public property. He himself laughed with his censors on the *ground* that he laughs best who laughs last. This annexation was the basis of President Lincoln's quotation that the ex-official was "Monarch of all he *surveyed*."

"Work, Work, Work is the Main Thing."

Abraham Lincoln's advice to a young man wishing to become a great lawyer. (1850).

No Day Without its Gain.

"I do not think much of a man who is not wiser to-day than he was yesterday."

All Nature a Mine.

"All nature, the whole world, material, moral, intellectual, is a mine."

Notes for a Lecture.

There is Another Great Man of that Name!

At the National Republican Convention, held at Philadelphia, on the 17th June, 1856, Abraham Lincoln was proposed as nominee for the Vice-Presidency. The first ballot produced for him 110 votes. The promising news reached him at Urbana, Ill., where he was attending court as a pleader. The telegram was so rare a feather for their townsman's cap that the cry arose: "He has become famous!" Lincoln read of the honor with incredulity, no doubt thinking that "there were strong men before Agamemnon," and remarked:

"There is a distinguished man of that name in Massachusetts."

Indeed, there was, the Governor of that State, Levi Lincoln, actually descended, like his namesake, from the Quaker Samuel Lincoln, of Hingham, Mass.

"Slavery is a Curse to the White Man."

"We will speak for freedom and against slavery, until everywhere, on this wide land, the sun shall shine, and the rain shall fall, and the wind shall blow upon no man who goes forth to unrequited toil. . . . Slavery is a curse to the white man, wherever it has existed."

Speech at Charleston, Ill., 1856.

"Slavery is Wrong!"

The author proclaimed this sentiment as the profound central truth of the Republican party; the whole paragraph is:

"Slavery is wrong, and ought to be dealt with as wrong."

Speech at Springfield, Ill., June, 1858.

"No Man Good Enough to Govern Another."

"I say that no man is good enough to govern another man without that other man's consent. I say this is the leading principle, the sheet-anchor of American Republicanism."

No Moon, No Murder.

In 1858, Lincoln was engaged in the campaign for the senatorship which later lifted him into his candidacy for the Presidency. But in spite of his having for the sake of this contest relinquished for the time the practice of law, he acquiesced in an appeal for him to speak in the defence of the son of an old neighbor of Sangamon County, accused of murder. This Armstrong had been "mixed up" with some fighters, and, as one of them died from a blow, the conspiring witnesses of the "chance-medley" affirmed that the blow was struck with an instrument in the accused man's hands. On the morning of the trial Lincoln said to the mother of the prisoner, "Your son will be free before sundown," and such was the local faith in "Honest Abe" that she awaited the result with lessened anxiety.

Lincoln had sifted out the evidence so that the sole dangerous point was from one witness, who persisted in repeating positively that he had seen the fatal blow struck, and declared the weapon to have been a slung-shot.

Question.—"How could you have seen him strike the fatal blow when, according to all the evidence, the quarrel occurred

5

between eleven and twelve o'clock at night, when there was no light of any kind?"

The man quickly replied: "I saw it by the light of the moon, which was shining brightly."

This seemed decisive, but the advocate, prepared at all points, said:

"Gentlemen of the jury, I hold in my hand the proof that on the night of the supposed murder *there was no moon* in the sky!"

He produced the almanac to convince the court, and the man was released to gladden his mother. Lincoln refused any fee for this service to a neighbor.

Make a Man Beat Himself.

On the eve of the first of the tilts in the demagogical debate of Lincoln and Douglas, a friend of the former assured him that he would beat the more practised orator and obtain the senatorship if he made the best use of his opportunity.

"No," was the answer. "I can't beat him for the Senate, but I 'll make him beat himself for the Presidency."

"But," adds Mr. Leonard Swett, who recounts the prophecy, "at that moment Lincoln had no more idea of being nominated for and elected to that office [the Presidency] than of being crowned Emperor of China."

Mrs. Lincoln, however, had the thought twenty years earlier.

Make Marks not to be Forgotten.

The Douglas-Lincoln debates fixed the slavery problem as "the great and durable question of the age." Lincoln also thought that the destinies of the nation might hang upon it. In referring to that electioneering duel he said:

"Though I now sink out of view and shall be forgotten, I believe I have made some marks which will tell for the cause of civil liberty long after I am gone."

"Revolutionize Through the Ballot-Box."

Although Lincoln espoused the cause of freedom, he did not at once side with the extremists, and he was incorrectly ranked in 1858 with the Abolitionists. Indeed, he said flatly at the time of that agitation:

"Let there be peace! Revolutionize through the ballot-box; and restore the Government once more to the affections and hearts of men by making it express, as it was intended to do, the highest spirit of justice and liberty."

"Win, or Die A-Trying!"

When Judge H. W. Beckwith, of Danville, came over to Ottawa, where the debates were to begin to which Lincoln had challenged his opposing candidate, Stephen A. Douglas, he found his friend looking careworn. Douglas had at first rejected the challenge, but later accepted it. His supporters and not a few of the

Lincolnites supposed that the first encounter would see "the Little Giant" (Douglas was a stumpy, thick-set man, like Daniel Webster in miniature) "*chaw up* Old Abe."

But Lincoln threw off his sombreness and, accosting Mr. Beckwith with his old free and easy manner, asked after friends where he "hailed from," and, with a certain familiar abruptness not unusual in him, said:

"Come sit down, and I will tell you a story." He began by repeating something like the passage in Crockett's *Memoirs*, accepted at that time in the West as realistic, of the boy fighting a fist-fight in the woods, and added:

"You see, the other fellow is not saying a word. His arms are at his side, his fists are closely doubled up, his head is drawn to the shoulder, and his teeth are set firmly together. *He* is saving his wind for the fight, and, as sure as it comes off, he will win it, or die a-trying."

Inferable Evidence.

In June, 1858, in the first of the Douglas-Lincoln debates, the latter cited, in reference to the Kansas-Nebraska Act, the proceedings under it by Presidents Franklin Pierce and James Buchanan, and the Dred Scott decision by Chief Justice Roger B. Taney, as resembling the frame of a house:

"When we see a lot of framed timbers, different portions of which we know have been gotten out at different times and places and by different wormmen,—Stephen, Franklin, Roger, and James, for instance,—and we see these timbers joined together, and see they exactly make the frame of a house or a mill, all the tenons and mortises exactly fitting, and all the lengths and proportions of the different pieces exactly adapted to their respective places, and not a piece too many or too few, not omitting even scaffolding—or, if a single piece be lacking, we see the place in the frame exactly fitted and prepared yet to bring such a piece in—in such a case we find it impossible not to believe that *Stephen* and *Franklin* and *Roger* and *James* all understood one another from the beginning, and all worked upon a common plan or draft, drawn up before the first blow was struck."

A House Divided Cannot Stand.

It was in this speech that Lincoln used the famous symbol of the "house divided against itself," which gave the key to the campaign he proposed—"A house divided against itself cannot stand. I believe this Government cannot endure permanently half slave and half free. . . . I do not expect the house to fall, but I do expect it will cease to be divided. It will become all one thing or all the other."

When his friends and advisers objected to his using the expression of the "divided house," Lincoln said:

"That expression is a truth of all experience. The proposition is indisputably true, and has been true for more than six thousand years, and—I will deliver this speech as it is written. I would rather be defeated with this expression in the speech than be victorious without it."

Asked again, later, to recall his statement or to revise it, he replied:

"If I had to draw a pen across my record and erase my whole life from sight, and I had one poor gift or choice left as to what I should save from the wreck, I should choose that speech and leave it to the world unerased."

Easier to Make a New Speech than an Old One.

In the discussions of 1858, it was noticed that Douglas clinched his nails of rhetoric by repeated blows, while the younger contestant seldom repeated his images and allusions. It was a question of fertility of invention and of resources, like the composer Rossini, who, when writing an opera in bed, preferred to compose an entire *aria* to getting off the couch and seeking some leaves which had blown beneath it.

Practice Before and Behind the Bar.

The Rev. Dr. Cuyler has cited Abraham Lincoln among the illustrious upholders of 'temperance and is justified in so doing. This does not conflict with the fact that the village stores with which Lincoln was connected as assistant and proprietor in his earlier years were groggeries as well as groceries—it was inevitable at the time. The bar was as set a fixture as the counter. Rum and whiskey were the two medicines most generally used. The ex-bartender did not deny the fact although it was a light stigma to bear. Nevertheless, in the Douglas-Lincoln debates, the former had the unkindness to utter a slur about his adversary having more practice behind the bar than before it—for Lincoln had but recently been admitted to plead in the courts. It was an allusion capable of happy retort. It was a common cry that Judge and Senator Douglas was a "*judge* of good liquor," as the saying goes. It was the era of good living, when Martin Van Buren was a "*prince* of good fellows."

"This," returned Lincoln with his incipient wink to accentuate the humor, "applies with similar force to my dignified opponent, as, while I have practised behind the bar, he has practised *before it!*"

No Cabbages Sprouting on My Face.

It was probably the contrast in the personal aspect of the champions of the Democratic and the Republican parties in 1858, in Illinois, that infused noticeable ıeat into the utterances of both orators ınd that piqued the hearers; and, as the ·unior disputant pointed out, their ca-·eers were unlike in progress and fruit.

"With me," said Abraham Lincoln, ' the race of ambition has been a flat fail-ıre. [He had failed in a late election.] Vith Mr. Douglas, it has been one of plendid success. . . . All the anxious ›oliticians of his party have been looking ıpon him as certain to be the President ›f the United States. They have seen n his jolly, round, fruitful face, post-›ffices, land-offices, marshalships, and Cabinet appointments, *chargé*-ships and oreign missions, bursting and sprouting ›ut, in wonderful exuberance, ready to be aid hold of by their greedy hands. And as hey have been gazing upon this attractive ›icture so long, they cannot . . . bring hemselves to give up the charming hope; ›ut, with greedier anxiety, they rush ıbout him, sustain him and give him narches, triumphal entries, and receptions beyond what even in the days o his highest prosperity they could hav brought about in his favor.

"On the contrary, nobody has eve expected *me* to be President. In m poor, lean, lank face, nobody has eve seen that *any cabbages were sproutin out!* These are disadvantages . . that the Republicans labor under. W have to fight this battle upon principle and upon principle alone."

The pain and pitifulness of this self depreciation lie in its truth—the Ugl Duckling knew his physical imperfec tions æsthetically and jested at them.

"No Royalty in Our Carriage."

Although in 1858 there were neithe Wagner nor Pullman cars, a special trai was provided for Senator Douglas, whil Lincoln was consigned to an ordinary one Once, when the decorated coache flaunted by, the lowly candidate, side tracked in a freight train, said:

" The gentleman in that turnout evi-ently smelt no royalty in our carriage ! "

" Hold My Coat while I Stone Stephen ! "

In the debate between Douglas and .incoln, in 1858, the former, a practised nd popular demagogue, led off with so aptivating a discourse that his oppo-ent's adherents believed the battle was 'on and that their spokesman would not ave a hearing from the enthralled crowd. ;ut Lincoln got up as soon only as the heers died away, looking taller and iore angular than ever, and " shucking " is long linen duster, which he dropped n the arm of a young bystander, re-iarked in his piping voice, which never-ieless had a far-pervading tone:
" Hold my coat while I *stone Stephen !* "

This pun annulled the good effect of ie previous harangue, and the disputant 'as listened to with attention.

It is interesting to recall that the two contestants should in youth have been rivals for the hand of the same woman. A further incident in their relations may be noted: At the inauguration of Lincoln, Douglas had the courtesy to hold Lincoln's hat. Moreover, the "Roger" of the episode recorded on page 70, administered the oath of office, while the "James" also cited was the retiring President, Buchanan.

Familiarize with Chains and You Prepare to Wear Them.

"Our reliance [against tyranny] is the love of liberty which God has planted in us. Our defence is in the spirit which prizes liberty as the heritage of all men, in all lands—everywhere. Destroy this spirit and you have planted the seeds of despotism at your own doors. Familiarize yourselves with the chains of bondage and you prepare your own limbs to wear them.

Accustomed to trample on the rights of others, you have lost the genius of your own independence, and become fit subjects of the first cunning tyrant who rises among you."

Speech at Edwardsville, Ill., Sept. 13, 1858.

Fighting Proves Nothing.

"I am informed that my distinguished friend [Douglas] yesterday became a little excited—nervous perhaps,—and said something about *fighting*, as though referring to a pugilistic encounter between him and myself. . . . Well, I merely wish to say that I shall fight neither Judge Douglas nor his second. . . . In the first place, a fight would prove *nothing* which is in issue in this contest. . . . If my fighting Judge Douglas would not prove anything, it would certainly prove nothing for me to fight his bottle-holder. My second reason . . . is that I don't believe the Judge wants it himself. He and I are about the best friends in the world, and when we get together, he would no more think of fighting me than of fighting his wife. Therefore, when the Judge talked about fighting, he was not giving vent to any ill feeling of his own, but merely trying to excite—well, *enthusiasm* against me on the part of his audience. And as I find he was tolerably successful, we will call it quits."

Speech at Havana, Ill., 1858.

"Return to the Fountain!"

"My countrymen, if you have been taught doctrines conflicting with the great landmarks of the Declaration of Independence; if you have listened to suggestions which would take away from its grandeur and mutilate the fair symmetry of its proportions; if you have been inclined to believe that all men are not created equal in those inalienable rights enumerated in our chart of liberty, let me entreat you to come back! Return to the Fountain whose waters spring close by the blood of the Revolution. You may do anything with me you choose, if you will but heed these sacred principles. I charge you to drop every paltry and insignificant thought for any man's success. It is nothing; I am nothing; Judge Douglas is nothing. But do not destroy that immortal emblem of humanity—the Declaration of Independence."

Speech at Beardsville, Ill., Aug. 12, 1858. Characterized by Horace White, reporting it for the Chicago *Tribune,* as Lincoln's "greatest inspiration."

The Bulwark of Liberty.

"What constitutes the bulwark of our liberty and independence? It is not our frowning battlements, our bustling seacoasts, our army and our navy. These are not our reliance against tyranny. Our reliance is the love of liberty which God has planted in us."

Speech at Edwardsville, Ill., Sept. 13, 1858.

"The Boy Who Did not Weigh as Much as Expected, and He Knew He Would n't!"

In the Douglas-Lincoln debates, a flurry was originated by a trick—fair enough perhaps as matters are in "love, war and politics." Resolutions adopted by a "hole-in-a-corner" meeting of Abolitionists were attributed to a council at which Lincoln was, furthermore, accused of presiding. The assertion, when disproved, greatly injured the Democratic cause. Horace Greeley, in a style quite Lincolnic, wrote on this blunder:

"Douglas is like the man's boy who did not weigh as much as he expected, and he always knew he would n't." [1] Lincoln capped the slip by doubting the genuineness of a document which his adversary produced—after the Springfield "forgery!"

Playing Cuttlefish.

"Judge Douglas is *playing cuttlefish*—a *small* species of fish that has no mode of defending itself when pursued, except by throwing out a black fluid which makes the water so dark the enemy cannot see it; and thus it escapes."

Speech at Charleston, Ill., 1858.

"The Eternal Struggle between Right and Wrong."

"Slavery is the real issue. It will continue in this country when these poor

---

[1] The paragraph Greeley misquoted was thus printed in 1838. DEFINITE INFORMATION—"Well, Robert, how much did your pig weigh?" "It did not weigh as much as I *expected*, and I always thought it *would n't*."—*Detroit Spectator*.

tongues of Judge Douglas and myself shall be silent. It is the eternal struggle between two principles—Right and Wrong—throughout the world. . . . The one is the common right of humanity, and the other the divine right of kings. . . . It is the same spirit that says:

" 'You work and toil and earn bread—and I 'll eat it!'

" No matter in what shape it comes, whether from the mouth of a king who seeks to bestride the people of his own nation and live by the fruit of their labor, or from one race of men as an apology for enslaving another race, it is the same tyrannical principal."

Last debate between Douglas and Lincoln, 1858.

Atalanta and the Apple.

Lincoln lost the prize of the senatorship of Illinois to his personal and political antagonist, Stephen A. Douglas, by persisting in a course in regard to slavery which was counter to the advice of his immediate friends. He related the following story to illustrate that he perfectly well knew what was at stake. He saw that while Douglas, a "trimmer," might win the lesser office, he would damn himself for the prospect of being the next President. It so fell out. The story runs in this guise:

"There was an old farmer out our way, who had a fair daughter and a fine apple-tree, each of which he prized as 'the apple of his eye.'

"One of the courters 'sparking' up for her hand was a dashing young fellow, while his rival next in consequence was but a plain person in face and speech, whom, however, the farmer favored, no doubt from 'Like liking Like.' (The dashing young chap was afterwards hanged, by the way.) One day, the two happened to meet at the farmer's fence. It enclosed his orchard where the famous Baldwin flourished. That year was the off-year, but, as somewhiles occurs, the yield, though sparse, comprised some rare beauties. There was one, a 'whopper,' on which the farmer had centred his care as if for a human pet. He looked after it well, and saw it heave up into plumpness with joy. When Dashing Jack came up, he saw his fellow-beau just hefting a stone.

"'What are you going to do with that rock?' asked he, careless-like, though somehow or other interested, too, as we are in anything a rival does in the neighborhood of our sweetheart.

"'Why, I was just a-going to see if I could knock off that big red apple, that is all.'

"'You can't do it in the first try!' taunted the dasher.

"'Neither can you. Bet!'

"Jack would not make any bet with plain John, but he took up a pebble and, contemptously whistling through his fine regular teeth, shied, and, sure as fate!

knocked the big Baldwin in the girth and sent it hopping off the limb. Then, as the victors are entitled to the spoil, he went in, picked up the fruit, and was walking up to the house when whom should he run up against but the old man! Now, to see *that* apple off, and to see any man munching it like a crab, was too much for his nerves. He did not stop to say 'Meal or Flour?' but, wearing these here copper-toed boots such as were a novelty in that section 'bout then, he raised the young man so that he and the apple, to which he clung, landed on this side of the fence together, in two-two's.

"Then? well! then, the plain John swallowed a snicker or two, and went right in, condoled with the old fellow on his loss of the pet Baldy, and asked for the girl right slick.

"Dashing Jack got the apple, but it was t' other *who got the gal.*"

Truly, Douglas secured the senatorship, but Lincoln won the Presidency.

(Another version substitutes a pear for the apple, but the gist is the same and the application thereof.)

"After Larger Game."

In the debates of 1858, Lincoln had impaled his adversary on the dilemma: "Could a Territory exclude slavery prior to a State constitution?" If Douglas said "No" he would offend the Illinois people and would lose the local prize; if he said "Yes," he would offend the South and lose their votes in the coming Presidential election. Douglas answered evasively. He won the place in Washington for the time, but his "Freeport doctrine," or "unfriendly legislation," prohibited his carrying the South in the greater contest.

In 1860, when Lincoln had won the stake for which his rival had been playing, a friend recalled that, when the weapons were forged, he had objected to this very one because it wounded the hand that made it, and sagely added:

"We were both right, for the question lost Douglas the Presidency but lost you the senatorship."

"I was after larger game," remarked the President.

Demonstration More than Proof and Reason.

"In the course of my law reading, I constantly came upon the word 'demonstrate.' I thought, at first, that I understood its meaning, but soon became satisfied that I did not. I said to myself: What do I mean when I 'demonstrate' more than when I 'reason' or 'prove'? How does 'demonstration' differ from any other proof? I consulted all the dictionaries and books of reference I could find, but with no better result. You might as well have defined 'blue' to a blind man. At last, I said: Lincoln, you can never make a lawyer, if you do not understand what 'demonstrate' means. I left my situation [law clerk] at Springfield, went home to my father's house, and stayed there until I could give any proposition in the Six Books of Euclid at sight. I then found out what 'demonstrate' means."

Lincoln, to Dr. Gulliver, of Norwich, Conn., 1859.

No Surrender.

"The cause of civil liberty must not be surrendered at the end of one or of a hundred defeats!"

[*Letter* to Chairman Judd, Republican Convention, 1859.]

American Public Opinion.

"Public opinion in this country is everything."

Speech in Ohio, 1859.

Natural Perpetual Motion.

"The mammoth and the mastodon have gazed on Niagara. In that long, long time, never still for a single moment, never dried, frozen, slept, or rested."

Notes for a Lecture, 1859.

(Alas! In fifty years, Niagara is threatened to be a dry bed, while the water, diverted for utilitarian uses, becomes but the tailraces of mills and factories. ("To what base uses we may *turn!*")

"The Plain People."

"I am most happy that the plain people understand and appreciate this."

Speech, in Ohio, 1859.

"Wealth Is a Superfluity of What We Don't Need."

President Lincoln to Locke ("Petroleum V. Nasby.")

"I Know that I am Right, because I Know that Liberty Is Right."

Said to Newton Bateman, Supt. Public Instruction, Illinois, 1860.

"Faith in God is Indispensable to Successful Statesmanship."

To N. Bateman, Supt. Public Instruction, Illinois, Nov., 1860.

"Understanded of the People."

Q.—"How did you get this unusual power of putting things clearly?

A.—"Among my earliest recollections, I remember how I used to get irritated when anybody talked to me in a way I could not understand. . . . I can remember going into my little bedroom, after hearing the neighbors talk with my father, and trying to make out what was the exact meaning of some of their—to me—dark sayings. I could not sleep when I got on such a hunt after an idea, until I had caught it; and when I thought I had got it, I was not satisfied until I had repeated it over and over, and had put it in language plain enough, as I thought, for any boy I knew to comprehend. This was a kind of passion with me, and it has stuck by me; for I am never easy now when I am *handling* a thought till I have bounded it north, and bounded it south, and bounded it east, and bounded it west."

To Dr. Gulliver, Norwich, Conn., 1859.

The Ideal Income in the Fifties.

On Lincoln's Eastern tour, with the view of making him known outside of his "section," he visited New York. Meeting another of "the Illini," who had prospered, and who told him that he had made a hundred thousand dollars, Lincoln observed:

"I have the cottage [a two-story wooden frame house, with extension, eight rooms] in Springfield, and about eight thousand dollars in money. If they make me Vice-President with Seward, as some say they will, I hope I shall be able to increase it to twenty thousand; and that is as much as any man ought to want."

"Right makes Might."

"Let us have faith that right makes might; and in that faith let us, to the end, dare to do our duty as we understand it."

Speech at Cooper Institute, N. Y., 1860.

"Cæsar an' Pompey Berry much Alike—'Specially Pompey!"

"I have no prejudice against the Southern people. They are just what we should be in their situation. If slavery did not now exist among them they would not introduce it. If it did now exist among us we should not instantly give it up."

The Lincoln–Hamlin Anagram.

At the time of the election of the Presidential ticket comprising Lincoln and Hannibal Hamlin, it was noted that the combination of the two names presented a peculiar result.

For instance:

Ham Lin
Lin Coln

Read up and down and then across.

Now, again:

Abra-Hamlin-Coln

Can you find two other names of two other men whose official lives and whose names combine as these do?

Whiskers, or No Votes!

Towards the end of his first Presidential campaign, Lincoln, who had always been clean-shaven, a fashion which was pretty general in the fifties, astonished his friends by growing the hirsute adornment seen in his latest photographs. Asked by an intimate friend what had induced the adoption of the new mode, he answered:

"Two young ladies at Buffalo wrote me that they wanted their fathers and beaux to vote for me, but I was so homely-looking that the men refused. The ladies insisted that if I would only grow whiskers it would improve my appearance, and I would get four more votes! So I grew whiskers."

Told by Mr. J. H. Littlefield.

Rather be Assassinated than Surrender Equal Rights.

These prophetic lines appear in the speech of the President-elect made at Independence Hall, Philadelphia, on the 22d of February, 1861:

"But if this country cannot be saved without giving up that principle [of equal rights], I was about to say I would rather be assassinated on this spot than surrender it."

(The plot, through apprehension of which the President was induced to enter the seat of Government surreptitiously, is now believed to have been a deception.)

"A Hard Nut to Crack."

"The authors of the Declaration of Independence meant it to be—as, thank God, it is now proving itself—a stumbling-block to those who in after times might seek to turn a free people back into the hateful paths of despotism. They knew the proneness of prosperity to breed tyrants, and they meant when such should reappear in this fair land and commence their vocation they should find left at least one hard nut to crack."

The Chorus of the Union.

(*To the Southern States*:)

"We are not enemies, but friends. We

must not be enemies. Though passion may have strained, it must not break our bonds of affection. The mystic chords of memory, stretching from every battle-field and patriot grave to every living heart and hearthstone all over this broad land, will yet swell the chorus of the Union, when again touched, as surely they will be, by the better angels of our nature."

First Inaugural Address, March 4, 1861.

Take Time!

"Nothing valuable can be lost by taking time."

Inaugural Address, 1861.

The People Are the Rightful Masters.

"Unless my rightful masters, the American people, shall withhold the requisite means or direct the contrary."

Inaugural Address, 1861.

Owners of Our Country.

"This country, with its institutions, belongs to the people who inhabit it."

Inaugural Address, 1861.

Confidence in Popular Justice.

"Why should there not be a patient confidence in the ultimate justice of the people."

Inaugural Address, 1861.

My War.

One of the slanders current during the outset of the civil strife was that the President was merely the figure-head behind which the Cabinet officers exercised, in each capacity, an autocracy. But the facts have since proved that nearly every important act had the initiative in Lincoln's brain, and nearly all the manifestation in force from his hand. In the annual report of Secretary Cameron, the advice was promulgated that the slaves should be armed in order to rise successfully against their masters—an idea embodied in the Emancipation Act, long held in abeyance by the President. When the latter came to that paragraph in the report, he scratched it out with his pen, indignantly remarking:

"This is a question which belongs exclusively to me."

Letting Rooms in a House Afire!

After his inauguration, President Lincoln was so continuously beset by office-seekers that he was almost compelled to neglect measures for the preservation of the Union. "If this keeps on," said he, "I shall be like a man who is busy letting lodgings at one end of his house while the other end is afire."

"Accuse not a Servant to his Master."

Lincoln's accessibility resembled that of the Oriental potentates, enjoined by their religion to hear all comers. Like them, too, he was mainly approached by persons with grievances, presented with a view of displacing some one from office that the complainant might be benefited. Lincoln once told an interested denouncer of this type to go home and read "Proverbs xiii., 10." On consulting the book the man found these words:

"Accuse not a servant to his master, lest he curse thee, and thou be found guilty."

Either Prince or Premier must be Puppet.

It was a curious fact that W. H. Seward was proposed as candidate for the Presidency in 1860, with Abraham Lincoln as his Vice-President. Consequently, the former had prepared himself for the foremost position and, no doubt, it harmonized with his disposition, when made Lincoln's Secretary of State, to have to compose, according to tradition, the speeches to foreign ministers and even to home delegations. He furnished such a paper for the reception of the Swiss Minister, and sent it by messenger to the Chief's hands, who received it as he was chatting with some friends. He glanced at the document, and, raising his voice to imply that here was no state secret, said:

"Oh, this is a speech Mr. Seward has written for me, eh? I guess I may try it before these gentlemen, and see how it will go." He read it with that spirit of burlesque in which, twenty years before, when a Congressman, he was wont to regale the boarding-house table with a parody of the members' "speechifying," and concluded: "There, *I* like it! It has the merit of originality!"

(Fortunately, his speeches were of his own emanation, and not in the character of the autograph of "John Phœnix," "which could be relied on as genuine, as it was written for him by one of his most intimate friends!")

When Generals were in Excess.

At the outset of the Civil War, military titles and promotions were the fruit of political energy. The Chief of State merrily said that he had made so many brigadier-generals for non-military purposes that you could hardly throw a stone about the capital without hitting one. (The N. Y. *Mercury* correspondent corroborates this statement in his communication to the War Bureau that at any hour a regiment could be formed at Willard's Hotel bar composed entirely of officers.)

Sorry to Lose the Charger.

A friend of a brigadier-general who had been captured by the enemy, horse, boots, and saddle, was thus condoled with by the President:

"I am sorry about the horse."

"What do you mean, sir?"

"Only that I can get a brigadier-general any day—they are more plentiful than drum-majors—but those horses cost the Government a hundred and twenty dollars a head!"

"File It Away in the Stove."[1]

Secretary of War Stanton was both naturally and, by virtue of his office, bellicose, and when pestered by a swarm of annoyances his temper was often carried to a high point. One day, he complained to President Lincoln of a major-general, who had accused him of favoritism in grossly abusive terms. His auditor advised him to write a sharp rejoinder.

"Prick him hard!" were the words.

Mr. Stanton read the draft surcharged by this backing, while the hearer kept favorably commenting:

---

[1] Readers of "Mark Twain's" writings during the War, will recall his expressed belief that communications to Government officials at Washington were "filed away in the stove." Was this a coincidence or a Lincoln echo?

"Right! just it! score him deeply! That's first rate, Stanton!"

But when the gratified author began folding up the paper to fit into an envelope the counsellor interrupted with:

"What are you going to do with it now?"

The Secretary was about to despatch it, of course.

"Nonsense," said the President, "you don't want to send that letter. *Put it in the stove!* That's the way I do when I have written a letter while I am mad. It is a good letter, and you've had a good time writing it, and feel better. Now, burn it, and write again."

Logic is Logic.

At a ball at the White House, thieves made off with many of the hats and overcoats of the guests, so that, when ready to take leave, Vice-President Hamlin's head covering was not to be found.

"I'll tell you what, Hamlin," said a

friend; "early in the evening I saw a man, possessed of keen foresight, hide *his* hat up-stairs. I am sure he would be willing to donate it to the administration, and I will go and get it for you."

When the hat was produced it was found to be very much after the style affected by Hamlin, but it bore a badge of mourning, which emblem the Vice-President ripped off with his penknife. The party stood chatting merrily as they waited for the carriages to be driven up, when a man stepped directly in front of Mr. Hamlin and stood staring at the "tile" with which his head was covered.

"What are you looking at, sir?" asked Hamlin sharply.

"Your hat," answered the man mildly. "If it had a weed on it, I should say it was mine."

"Well, it has n't got a weed on it, has it?" asked the Vice-President.

"No, sir," said the hatless man, "it has n't."

"Then it is n't your hat, is it?" said the proud possessor of it.

"No, I guess not," said the man as he turned to walk away. When this little scene was explained to President Lincoln, he laughed heartily and said:

"That reminds me, Hamlin, of 'the stub-tailed cow.'

"It was a long time ago, when I was pioneering and soldiering in Illinois [1832], and we put up a joke on some officers of the United States Army. My party and I were a long way off from the comforts of civilized life, and our only neighbors were the garrison of a United States fort. We did pretty well for rations, had plenty of salt meat and flour, but milk was not to be had for love or money; and as we all longed for the delicacy, we thought it pretty mean that the officers of the fort, who had two cows—a stubbed-tailed one and a black and white one—offered us no milk, though we threw out many and strong hints that it would be acceptable. At last, after much consultation, we decided to teach them a lesson and to borrow or steal one of those cows, just as you choose to put it. But how it could be done without the cow being at once identified and recovered was the question.

"At last we hit on a plan. One of our party was despatched a day's ride to the nearest slaughter-house, where he procured a long red cow's tail to match the color of the stub-tailed cow, after possessing ourselves of which animal we neatly tied our purchase to the poor stub, and with appetites whetted by long abstinence we drank and relished the sweet milk which 'our cow' gave. A few days afterward we were honored by a call from the commander of the fort.

"'Say, boys,' said he, 'we have lost one of our cows.' Of course we felt very sorry and expressed our regret accordingly. 'But,' continued the commander, 'I came over to say that if that cow of yours had a stub tail, I should say it was ours.'

"'But she has n't a stub tail, has she?" asked we, sure of our point.

"'No,' said the officer, 'she certainly has not a stub tail.'

"'Well, she is n't your cow then,' and our argument was unanswerable as was Hamlin."

Tell a Horse's Points, not how Many Hairs in his Tail.

So voluminous a report was made by a Congressional committee upon a new gun that the President pathetically said: "I should want a new lease of life to read this through. Why cannot an investigatory committee occasionally exhibit a grain of common sense? If I send a man to buy a horse for me, I expect to have him tell me his points, and not how many hairs he has on his tail."

An Evasive Answer.

A committee of Kentuckians went to see Abraham Lincoln in 1861, with reference to the abolition of slavery. Many Kentuckians owned slaves. They were anxious to remain in the Union, but they did not want to lose their bondmen. The spokesman of the party was a tall man of about Lincoln's height. He made an eloquent speech, filled with fine sentiments and flowery metaphor, and closed with a crashing peroration. After he had finished, Lincoln looked at him a moment and then said quietly: "Judge, I believe your legs are as long as mine."

"A Little More Light and a Little Less Noise!"

At the outset of the war, when the campaign was conducted coincidently by the chief newspapers, a correspondent of a New York journal called to propose still another plan to the plan-ridden President, who listened patiently, then said:

"Your New York papers remind me of a little story.

"Some years ago, there was a gentleman travelling through Kansas on horseback. There were few settlements and no roads, and he lost his way. To make matters worse, as night came on, a terrific thunderstorm arose, and peal on peal of thunder, following flashes of lightning, shook the earth or momentarily illuminated the scene. The terrified traveller then got off and led his horse, seeking to guide it as best he might by the flickering light of the quick flashes of lightning. All of a sudden, a tremendous crash of thunder brought the man to his knees in terror, and he cried out:

"'O Lord! if it's all the same to you give us a little more light and a little less noise!'"

Take One from Three and—None Remain.

In April, 1861, the patriot statesmen of the North were in a state of anxiety, as the least precipitate act might cause the wavering border States, such as Tennessee, Kentucky, and Missouri, to throw in their fortunes with the Carolinas, Georgia, Florida, Mississippi, and Arkansas. Nevertheless, a deputation, boiling over with impatience arising from patriotic wrath, urged the President to do something at once.

He replied with apparent irrelevance:

"If you fire at three pigeons on a rail, and you kill one, how many will be left?"

There was no delay in the answer: "Two!"

"Oh, no," corrected he; "there would be none left; for the other two, frightened by the shot, would have flown away."

Labor and Capital.

"I ask a brief attention. It is to the effort to place capital on an equal footing with, if not above, labor in the structure of government. It is assumed that labor is available only in connection with capital; that nobody labors unless somebody lse owning capital somehow, by the use f it, induces him to labor. Labor is prior o and independent of capital. Capital s only the fruit of labor, and could never ave existed if labor had not first existed. abor is the superior of capital, and de- erves much the higher consideration."

Presidential Message, 1861.

How Long a Man's Legs Should Be.

The shortest President was William I. Harrison, and the tallest was Abraham incoln. It was *not* the former, how- ver, who put the question of how long a nan's legs should be, but some impertinent ack-a-dandy at a levee. The reply he eceived was as follows:

" A man's legs should be long enough o reach from his body to the ground."

What is Done for Others We Think on Most Pleasantly.

In the fall of 1861, in behalf of a young Vermont soldier condemned to death for sleeping on post, Mr. Chittenden, a government officer, appealed first to the Secretary of War and finally to the President for the life of the youngster. One of the complaints of the martinets was that, on account of his merciful intercessions, the President was a poor Commander-in-chief. In this case, however, he promised to suspend the execution and to act personally.

Mr. Chittenden demurred at imposing another burden on an over-burdened man.

"Never mind," said Lincoln. "Scott's life is as valuable to him as that of any person in the land. You remember the remark of the Scotchman about the head of a nobleman who was beheaded:

"'It was no great head, but it was the only one he had.'"[1]

The Vermonter was released and won

[1] In the original story it is a Scotchwoman in the Highlands lamenting the decapitation of her laird. "It waur na mitch o' a head, but, puir body! it waur a' the head the laird had."

promotion in his regiment, but he refused it. He died as a private, in action at Lee's Mills. With his latest breath he thanked the President who had allowed him to fall like a soldier. Of this valiant end Mr. Chittenden acquainted the benefactor, saying:

"I wish this matter could be written into history."

"None of that," broke in Lincoln. "You remember what Jeanie Deans said to the English Queen when begging for her sister's life:[1]

"'It is not when we sleep saft and wake merrily that we think o' ither people's sufferings; but when the hour of trouble comes, and when the hour of death comes—that comes to high and low—oh, then, it is n't what we have done for oursel's, but what we have done *for ithers* that we think on most pleasantly.'"

---

[1] *The Heart of Midlothian*, by Sir Walter Scott.

"No Blood on My Skirts."

One of the many stories showing the President's tenderness towards the class from which he had sprung is related by Mr. Thayer, who got it straight from a personal friend of Lincoln. The narrator had taken in hand the deliverance of a soldier, doomed to death for falling asleep on "sentry-go." Lincoln wrote the pardon, and remarked:

"It is not to be wondered at that a boy raised on a farm, probably in the habit of going to bed at dusk, should, when required to watch all night, fall asleep. I cannot consent to shoot him for such an act. I could not think of going into eternity with that poor young man's blood on my skirts."

The soldier was killed at Fredericksburg; and on his bosom was found a photograph of Lincoln with the legend: "God bless President Lincoln!"

It Does Not Hurt Me and Pleases Her.

In October, 1861, General Phelps, in taking possession of Ship Island, near New Orleans, issued a proclamation manumitting the slaves.[1] At this time, the President, while devoted to general freedom, was not committed to the wholesale liberation. Yet he took no official notice of the premature act. The matter being brought insistently before him, he finally rejoined:

"I feel about that a good deal as a man—whom I will call Jones—did about his wife. He was one of those meek men and had the reputaton of being 'henpecked.' At last, one day, his wife was

[1] When, later, General Frémont, commanding our army in the West, did a similar act, the President curbed him, stating that the Emancipation would be performed in due course, but by his own initiative. It was clear that not a few who aimed at the Presidential chair itched to hurl this thunderbolt.

seen switching him out of the house. A day or two afterwards, a friend met him on the street and said:

"'Jones, I 've always stood up for you, as you know, but I am not going to do it any longer. Any man who will stand quietly and take a switching from his wife deserves to be horsewhipped.'

"'Now, don't,' replies Jones, looking up with a wink and patting him on the back. 'Why, it did n't hurt me any, and you have no idea what a power of good it did Mary Ann.'"[1]

Stanton Murdered Sleep!

Contrary to the expectation of the "intelligent foreigner" who pried into our affairs when we were having our spring cleaning of traitors and the like parasites, it was not the Upstart from the West who

---

[1] The original story is told of an English "navvy," lusty and amply able to endure, whose wife was by comparison frail and feeble.

was the "Sir Anthony Absolute" of the capital, but Stanton, the Secretary of War. He was not always losing his temper, as he had never found it from the first slip immediately after *swearing* himself into office. He was the bogey of the swarm of political beggars, and a predestined buffer—not to say *chevaux-de-frise*—for the badgered President. "Go to Stanton" was in the latter's mouth what "Get thee into the Bastille!" was to King Louis XIV. of France. Lincoln said he got no rest between Stanton and the pesterers. "No government could sleep soundly while such a man as Secretary Stanton was stamping about in the corridors kicking chairs over and snapping bell cords." It was asserted that the imperious Anthony ruled the Cæsar; but the former's private secretary, who oftenest saw the two dignitaries together, totally denies this statement. At all events the superior had a high opinion of his lieutenant.

If Stanton Said So, It Must Be So!

A Western committee was referred to Secretary Stanton; he jeered at their scheme to transfer Western and Eastern troops for one another, and on hearing that the committee had the President's approval clinched his reply by averring disrespectfully:

"Then he is a dead-sure fool!"

This was repeated to the President, who pondered a while and then, looking up, merely said:

"If Stanton said I was a dead-sure fool, then I must be one, for Stanton is nearly always right and generally says what he means."

But, in the interest of peace, he nevertheless threw a sop to Cerberus, probably such a good story that even the Crying Philosopher would have laughed over it.

Told by Mr. G. W. Julian.

"Keep Silent, and We Will Get You Safe Across."

In the sixties, one of the most-talked-about of men was the French rope-walker, Blondin, who crossed Niagara Falls on a rope, often carrying a man on his back. On being asked why the living burden kept so absolutely immovable, he grimly replied: "I tell him if he move, and it is life or death for one or both, I shall drop him! So he cling tight!"

From the beginning of his occupation of the White House, Lincoln kept up the democratic tradition of "open house." Then began the endless stream of *clients*, which often angered the ushers and embarrassed the chief. On one occasion, after having listened with his unalterable patience to a delegation, the President said:

"That reminds me of Blondin the acrobat. Gentlemen, suppose all the property you were worth was in gold, and you had put it on the back of Blondin to carry across the Niagara River on a rope, would you shake the cable, or keep shouting to him:

" 'Blondin, stand up a little straighter! stoop a little more! lean a little more to the north! lean a little more to the south'?

"No, you would hold your breath as well as your tongue, and keep your hands off until he was safe over. The Government is carrying an immense weight. Untold treasures are in their hands. They are doing the best they can. Don't badger them. Keep silent, and we will get you safe across."

Name the Brand of Whiskey and I'll Send Some to All my Generals.

The actual course of events quite overcame the old wise saws in Washington when, like the capital of Judea, "the enemies had cast a trench about it, and compassed it round and kept it in on every side," while, likewise, threatening "to lay it even with the ground." Fault-finders and counsellors alike seemed as futile as the soldier-chiefs. Even when the news of the battle of Pittsburg Landing arrived, betokening a new light in the West, the cavillers still carped at "our only general," and belittled Grant by asserting that his spirit was due to being fortified by whiskey. His chief support, they had no hesitancy in declaring, was "leaning on the whiskey cask."

To a deputation of Prohibitionists, our "First Consul" blandly replied with affected eagerness:

"Gentlemen, if you can name the particular brand of whiskey General Grant uses I shall thank you, for I just want to send a barrel to every one of my other generals a-field."

Did His Work Well, but Always Squealed.

Secretary Stanton laid before the President some papers which appeared to show that a certain Northern war governor, while zealously supporting the cause and furthering it from his State's means and men, liked to do things in his own way. Thwarted in this, he was apt to impede movements which the chief military office intended to direct wholly.

The Executive read the documents, but did not share Mr. Stanton's apprehensions. On the contrary he smiled in his meaning way, and proceeded to say in his gentle, humorous voice:

"Your Governor reminds me of a boy whom I once saw at a launching. When a ship is ready to be launched, you know, the keel hangs on but by one point, where a 'dog' is to be knocked away. This was only a small concern, and, instead of a giant with a maul, a small boy was regularly employed to remove the *shore*. All he had to do was strike one smart blow, and lie right down in the hollow of the ways, whereupon the hull would slide clean over him in an instant. But the boy must needs begin to 'holler' as soon as the mass glided over him, and you would think by the yelling he was being murdered all the time of the passage. I myself thought the hide was being scraped from his back; but he was not hurt at all.

"The shipwright-boss told me that this lad was always chosen for the job, being 'peart' and spry, that he did his feat well, never had been grazed even, but that he *always* hollered in that way.

"Now, that's the way with our Governor Blank. He will do his work right enough, but he *must* squeal! We get good work; so let him do his squealing!"

Tackle One of Your Own Size.

P. T. Barnum, the showman, endeavored to repeat the success he had met with all over the world in his exhibition of "General Tom Thumb" by presenting another dwarf, "Commodore" Nutt. In 1862 they were at Washington, and in accordance with his usual method, in order to obtain a good advertisement from our uncrowned head, Barnum "engineered" it so that he should be invited to the White House with his celebrity. The Cabinet were assembled and the President introduced the Lilliputian to them. The manager relates:

"After a little joking Mr. Lincoln bent down his long, lank body, and taking Nutt by the hand said:

"'Commodore, permit me to give you a parting word of advice. When you are in command of your fleet, if you find yourself in danger of being taken prisoner, I advise you to *wade* ashore!'

"The commodore let his gaze travel up the whole length of Mr. Lincoln's extremely long legs, and replied, quietly:

"'I guess, Mr. President, *you* could do that better than *I* could!'"

"Butler or No Butler, Here Goes!"

Early in 1862, before General Butler

had entire sway at New Orleans, and was yet acquiring repute for inflexibility and independence, a soldier under his flag was condemned to death. The circumstances were such that his Congressman would not undertake the cause, and the Secretary of War, because of his severity, was deemed hopeless of approach by the grieving father who had hastened to the capital to endeavor to save his boy. In this dilemma, a passing sympathizer brought him into the Presidential presence, where he pleaded for his son's life. Unfortunately, the President had lately rectived a somewhat impertinent letter from General Butler, praying him not to interfere in cases of discipline, as it undermined the *morale* of the army. The announcement of this fact completed the mourner's distress, and his cry of anguish was so poignant that the President snatched up his pen and, with the ingenuity of a benevolent Machiavelli, wrote:

"J. S. is not to be shot until further orders from me."

"Butler or no Butler, here goes!" he added.

Through his streaming tears the trembling father could hardly read the precious lines, but then was aghast to find that he had not received a pardon.

Lincoln smiled at his fears and said:

"I see you are not acquainted with me, old friend. If your son never looks on death till further orders from me to shoot him, he will live to be a great deal older than old Methuselah!"

Such instances of his mercy, and of his belief that "shooting did no good to any man," were numerous.

No Going behind a Good Point.

Congressman Kellogg came before President Lincoln on behalf of the son of a constituent. The young man, after gallantry as a soldier, had fallen under condemnation. Extenuating circumstances also pleaded for him, but the hearer was most touched by the record of his being wounded under the flag.

" Kellogg, is there not something in the Bible about the shedding of blood remitting sins?"

The suitor assented.

" Well, that is a good point, and there 's no going behind it!" returned the arbiter, filling up and signing a pardon.

It was more evidence in favor of his truism that the burden of the war fell "most heavily on the soldier."

"How many Legs Will a Sheep Have?"

President Lincoln replied to a deputation, one of many urging immediate slave-emancipation when the proposition was not yet framed as a bill:

" If I issue a proclamation now, as you

suggest, it will be as ineffectual as the Pope's bull against the comet. It cannot be forced. Now, by way of illustration,—how many legs will a sheep have if you call his tail a leg?"

They all answered: "Five."

"You are mistaken, for calling a tail a leg does not make it so."

"Prayer and Praise Go Together."

In 1862, in the spring, the President suffered family bereavement and distress together with heart-rending news from the battle front, where the Union reverses were repeated. But at the very time when one son of Lincoln was laid to rest, and another was menaced with the same fate, the fall of Fort Donelson was reported. In his affliction, the father had been supported by a pious nurse who enjoined prayer upon him.

"There is nothing like prayer," she persisted.

Beaming with the unexpected good news, he replied:

"Yes, there is: praise! Prayer and praise must go together."

If I Were So Skeered I Should Go Home!

In March, 1862, the *Merrimac*, the first ironclad known, attacked and destroyed half of the U. S. Navy at Newport News.[1] The alarm among the monetary and mercantile classes was at first paralyzing,

[1] Early in 1862, there were rumors that a colossal engine of naval destruction was on the ways at Newport News; but though it was generally believed probable that the invention of a novelty in maritime warfare was quite possible by an intelligent people like our Southern brothers, the Government must have been misled either by want of, or by false information, and the rumor was mocked at in official circles. The *Merrimac* was not only a floating battery but had a ramming prow like those of ancient

but as soon as there was a revival of spirit, though not of courage, a deputation of New York financiers and merchants, representing untold wealth, hurried to the seat of government to demand of the Chief protection for the coast cities; the *Merrimac* was considered to be seaworthy.

"Gentlemen," said Lincoln, after regarding them and noting the evidences of rapid travel, their dismay at being near the battle-fields, and their expression of utter helplessness, "the Government has got no ship that I know of that can meet the *Merrimac*. [The *Monitor* was then

---

galleys. On Saturday, the 8th of March, 1862, this unknown construction revealed herself to the eyes of the Federal sentinels at Fortress Monroe, and the lookouts on the men-of-war under it saw "The Horror of the War" which was contrary to all ideas of naval craft. It was a low-lying hulk, covered with railroad iron so as to be bomb-proof and as stated, supplied with a beak to pierce, and by the immense weight behind it to crush in any obstacle encountered when under full speed. The ironclad steadily charged the blockading squadron, singling out an unknown quantity.] There is no money in the treasury, and our credit is none of the best. I don't know anything that we can do, but if I had as much money as you say you have, and I was as *skeered* as you are, I 'd go home and protect my own property."

Another version reads: "I 'd go home, build some war vessels, and present them to the Government." Old Commodore Vanderbilt had set the example by giving an ocean steamship.

---

the *Cumberland*, as most worthy of her prowess. She stood the frigate's broadsides without the least injury and rammed and sank the vessel in less than an hour. The *Congress* also struck her colors to the monster, and then the victor slowly retired. Consternation was left in her wake for nothing seemed able to beat off this new engine of war. The next day, however she was faced with another and more novel machine for ocean action, the *Monitor*.

While the rumors in regard to the formidable nature of the rebel ram *Merrimac*, were flying about, counter tales were circulated in New

He Furnished the Stone for the Sling.

Engineer Ericsson's plan for that novelty in naval warfare, the *Monitor,* was at first rejected by the Naval Board, but was upheld by President Lincoln, who maintained, against the opinion of the consulting engineers that the weight of armor was a matter of calculation. "On the Mississippi we used to figure to a pound what our flatboats and steamboats could carry." (He had built the former class with his own hands.)

When the dread *Merrimac*, rebel iron-clad ram, was understood to be about to

---

York about another strange vessel, built by Ericsson, the *Monitor*, which was hurried to the scene of action. The *Merrimac* came forth on Sunday morning to renew her terrible destruction, and a duel ensued between the two champions. The little "cheese-box on a plank," the invention of the famous Swede, with two guns only in the turret, bore the ponderous broadsides with immunity and finally forced a retreat. The insignificant stickle-back had ssue from port, at Newport News, on he offensive, and the *Monitor* was not yet ·eported, though at sea, the President ılone had faith in the latter.

"I believed in the *Monitor* when her lesigns were first shown me. I caught ;ome of the inventor's enthusiasm. I :hink she may be the veritable sling with :he stone to smite this Philistine *Merrimac* in the forehead."

The Confederate terror emerged, inflicted vast damage on the Federal fleet, and retired for a renewal of the struggle, or rather for further devastation. In the meantime the *Monitor* arrived, threw herself between ram and butt, and drove her giant adversary back into covert. "Throw but a stone—the monster dies!"

---

conquered the hippopotamus. The Confederate champion was disabled and had to be towed into Norfolk. From that day on, the type of the *Monitor*, with certain modifications, prevailed in naval construction. She was like the Circassion in his chain mail compared to the Crusader in massive plate armor.

The Assistant Secretary of the Navy acknowledged the inestimable debt to the inventor, Ericsson, and added that the credit for the actual construction of the terror-destroyer was entirely due to President Lincoln.

Take to the Woods!

The Spanish difficulty, which has popped up ever since there was an Expansion movement, arose during *the* War. Santo Domingo was then at daggers drawn and fleshed with Old Spain; and the Cabinet held a consultation upon the point whether we should aid the monarchy and, in a way, suppress the filibustering actions, or openly espouse the cause of colonial freedom. "Cuba free" was talked about, but even such expeditions as that of Lopez, which involved some of our daring citizens, had not implicated the Government. The Abolitionists, of course, sympathized with the revolted colony. The President was supposed to owe a great deal of his support to this class. Appealed to, he said:

"That reminds me of the negro at the camp-meeting. The preacher was, in his excitement, rather confused in his quotations. He cited the text as offering the two roads, saying: 'Dar are two roads afore ye, brethren: de narrer road, which leadeth to destruction; and de broad road, which leadeth right on to damnation!' 'In dat case' responded a hearer, rising to suit the action to the word, 'dis chile takes to de woods!'"

Hayti was recognized as an independent power, April, 1862, as had been done by Europe. The President advocated strict neutrality.

"Ain't We Glad to Git Out of the Wilderness!"

(*Popular negro minstrel song of the time.*)

In June, 1862, the daring cavalry raid by Colonel Stuart, around the Union army of McClellan, bringing Mars to the six-mile limit, threw the inhabitants of Washington into consternation. To a person of consequence who made anxious inquiries of the Chief, the latter replied with apprehension rarely shown by him:

"There is no news from the Army of the Potomac. I do not know whether we have any army!"

The interlocutor said fervently:

"If we do right, I believe that God will lead us safely out of the Wilderness,"—the usual designation of the brush tangle about the Potomac River Valley.

"My faith is greater than yours," rejoined Lincoln; "I, too, believe that if we do right God will lead us safely out of the Wilderness. I hope that a bright morning will follow this dark hour that now fills us with alarm. Indeed, my faith tells me it will be so." (The battle of Malvern Hill soon verified this faith.)

Recounted by ex-Senator Jas. F. Wilson.

"Be on the Lord's Side."

A member of the church, being at a Presidential reception, closed some remarks with the pious hope that the Lord would be "on our side."

"I am not at all concerned about that," commented the President, "for we know that the Lord is always on the side of the right. But it is my constant anxiety and prayer that I and this nation should be on the Lord's side."

Another Evasive Answer.

In the darkest hours of the Virginia campaign, July, 1862, a New York Democratic M. C., John Gannon, of Buffalo, who had supported the Republican Chief through thick and thin, deemed himself therefore privileged beyond all other inquisitors to receive intelligence of the movements of the army. The military situation was so critical that it was impossible for an outsider to be given any information. The President looked at Gannon a moment, and then, his eye catching the glint of the lustrous ivory front of the Congressman, whose face and forehead were as clean as a Chinaman's, returned:

"Gannon, how clean you shave!"

"A Private Has as Much Right to Justice as a Major-General."

Senator J. F. Wilson, in pleading the case of a soldier wrongfully accused of desertion, met with the cordial approbation of President Lincoln, but found the Secretary of War inexorable. The unflagging advocate re-appealed "to Caesar" and procured an over-riding order which the Secretary, after another protest, finally obeyed. On reporting the sequel to the Chief, the latter said:

"Well, I am glad you stuck to it, and that it ended as it did; for I meant it should so end if I had to give it personal attention. A private soldier has as nuch right to justice as a major-general."

True Intellectual Economy.

"I never let any idea escape me, but write it on a scrap of paper, and put it n a drawer. In that way I save my best thoughts on a subject, and such things often come in a kind of intuitive way more clearly than if one were to sit down and deliberately reason them out. To save the results of such mental action is true intellectual economy. It not only saves time and labor, but also the very best material the mind can supply for unexpected emergencies."[1]

Lincoln to Senator Wilson, 1862.

---

[1] An unconscious echo of this helpful hint to the art of composition is met with in Henri Mürger, author of *La Vie en Bohême*. The French author also impressed on his brothers of the pen the wisdom of keeping a common-place book, as the time would come when its reservoir of ideas "written out" would be invaluable to the man of letters. So, "great wits jump."

Cheering Not Military.

After the reverses of Bull Run, Aug. 2, 1862, the President went out to visit and encourage the soldiers. As he was about to review the command under Colonel (afterwards General) Sherman, the latter asked for a speech, but, in kindness to the civilian's ignorance, remarked that cheering was not military and that he hoped the orator would not draw out any boisterousness. The forces were raw recruits and were profoundly demoralized at the moment by a repulse, the vibration of which extended to Maine. According to Sherman, the speaker made "one of the neatest, best, and most feeling addresses ever listened to." The hearers were strongly inclined to cheer, but the President checked them with the dry, droll remark:

"Don't cheer, boys! I confess that I rather like it myself, but Colonel Sherman here says it is n't military; and I guess we had better defer to *his* opinion."

"Old Inflexible" Foreseen.

During the lax discipline at the outset of the war, a soldier ventured, in his superior's presence, to break ranks at a review and go up to the President and blurt out:

"Mr. President, I have a cause for grievance. I went to speak to Colonel Sherman, and he threatened to shoot me."

Repeating the charge, the hearer looked from the denunciator to the Colonel; then, bending his tall form towards the soldier, said in his thin, piping voice, which, however, always "carried well," so that the regiment overhead: "Well, if I were you, and Colonel Sherman had threatened to shoot *me,* I would n't *trust* him! for I believe he would do it!"

Save the Union!

"My paramount object in this struggle is to save the Union."

Rejoinder to Horace Greeley, Aug., 1862. On base of the Lincoln statue, Chicago.

"My Hope of Success Is in God's Justice and Goodness."

"My hope of success, in this great and terrible struggle, rests on that immovable foundation, the justice and goodness of God. And when events are very threatening, and prospects very dark, I still hope that all will be well in the end, because our cause is just and God is on our side."

To a deputation of clergy; the Rev. Dr. Gurley, present, the relater.

The Quiet Past Versus the Stormy Present.

"The dogmas of the quiet past are inadequate to the stormy present."

Presidential Message, Sept., 1862.

"The Union First and Foremost—Slavery Afterwards."

In Lincoln's letter to Horace Greeley, August 22, 1862, occurs the above passage demonstrating that the word had displaced the purse.

‘Freedom Is the Last, Best Hope of Earth!”

Presidential Message, Sept., 1862.

‘Who Would Be Free, Themselves Must Strike!”

“Disenthrall ourselves, and then we hall save ourselves.”

Presidential Message, Sept., 1862.

“We Cannot Escape History.”

Presidential Message, Sept., 1862.

The Butcher’s Bill.

“It is much, very much, that this would ost no blood at all.”

Message recommending the adoption of the resolutions concerning amnesty, of the united Houses, 1862.

“To Have Good Soldiers, Treat Them Rightly.”

Said to Senator Jas. F. Wilson, 1862.

A Rule Without Exception.

"When a man is sincerely penitent for his misdeeds, and gives satisfactory evidence of the same, he can safely be pardoned, and there is no exception to the rule."

Lincoln, as to his Amnesty Act.

What Use Is a Second Term to a Man Without a Country?

If there was any pang comparable to that experienced by President Lincoln when he suspended the Habeas Corpus Act it must have been when he consented to the Draft Act and imitated despotic rulers, in tearing the hopes and the props of the home from the roof-tree. But he did not flinch and when the new military chief, General Grant, asked for three hundred thousand men to "fight it out on that line though it took all summer," he could firmly state that he had called for *five* hundred thousand. It was then that he said in self-defence: "What use to me would be a second term if I had no country?"

One Dies but Once.

A widow woman of his early acquaintance approached Lincoln, when President, to renew the friendship, for he had saved her son from a false charge of murder without any expense, though it had cost him precious time during his campaign for the senatorship in 1858. Like a good many persons in the West, who had known him in his despondent period and who were superstitious, she shared in the belief which his stepmother had also entertained that he was not destined to live to a great age.

"Hannah Armstrong," he said, smiling, in his mysterious way, "if they *do* kill me, I shall never die another death!"

Lincoln's "Leg Cases."

When the people in Washington saw the lights burning late in the Executive

Mansion, though there was no Cabinet council, they would say, explanatorily, for the benefit of the stranger in the capital:

"That is the President, sitting up over private business. It is his great heart. He is trying to reconcile it with military duty, I guess,—going to try to let off some foolish or rash young fellow for the sake of his old folks."

There was, for example, the case of a deserter, whose old father sent a despatch to Senator Fessenden, pleading that he could shortly provide proofs that the young man was not an offender, but imploring time. The operator strove to discover the whereabouts of the senator, as he had not his address. On finding him and communicating the intelligence, the senator promptly hastened to the President, and had the satisfaction of "redeeming the captive" on the eve of execution.

Schuyler Colfax relates another of these

cases of clemency, but one which was not as deserving as the above. Judge Holt had the matter in hand and brought the papers to the President to have him sign the death-warrant. Lincoln's leniency was a football between himself and the War Department.

"This case," said the Judge, "is one which comes exactly within your requirements. The soldier does not deny his guilt; he will better serve the country dead than living, as he has no relations to mourn for him, and he is not fit to be in the ranks of patriots, at any rate." Mr. Lincoln's refuge of excuse was all swept away. Judge Holt expected, of course, that he would write "Approved" on the paper; but the President, running his long fingers through his hair, as he so often used to do when in anxious thought, replied, "Well, after all, Judge, I think I must put this with my leg cases."

"*Leg cases,*" said Judge Holt, with a frown at this supposed levity of the President, in a case of life or death. "What do you mean by *leg cases,* sir?"

"Why," replied Mr. Lincoln, "do you see these papers crowded into those pigeon-holes? They are the cases that you call by that long title, 'cowardice in the face of the enemy,' but I call them, for short, my 'leg cases.' But I put it to you, and I leave it for you to decide for yourself: If Almighty God gives a man a cowardly pair of legs how can he help their running away with him?"

How true was the ancient saying: "It is wise to know when to play the jester"!

This may remind one of the story told of King Henry of Navarre (Fourth of France) who, being seized with nervous trembling at the outset of a battle, cried to his staff: "Oh, cowardly custard of a body! do you quake now? I will take you to a hot corner where you will have something to shake for!" whereupon he spurred into the heat of the conflict with his quivering body.

"Don't Swap Horses Crossing the Stream."

In the troubled days when Washington and Richmond scowlingly confronted each other our "*Delenda est Carthago!*" resounded in the Senates on the Potomac and on the James. The fleeting show of commanders for the Union forces, a new head quickly replacing a decapitated chief, emboldened the wire-pullers who had a supply of round puppets for the square hole. Driven to the wall by this persistent sinning against the hallowed rule never to retire a general under the enemy's fire, the President, nominally generalissimo, replied to an importunate trumpeter of still another Bonaparte:

"There is a good old saying in the section of the country where I came from: 'Don't swap horses crossing the stream.'"

The story in detail is as follows:

Two men were travelling in the Blue Grass country where the rivers run bank-high during a freshet. They stopped at what was, in drier times, a ford. The clay had dyed the foaming waters the color of madder, and the crossing was only discernible to the mind's eye. Nevertheless, relying on the intelligence of their horses both men rode into the angry waters. When a third of the way over, the excellence of their mounts in battling with the obstacles encountered elicited frank expressions of praise. When halfway over, the animals still meriting eulogy, spite of pitfalls, mudholes, and "sawyers," they paused and, ignoring their fix, continued to praise their steeds. Only, each commended the *other's* property.

Totally unfit as was the time and the place for a "trade," they actually struck hands on an exchange of beasts and, what was more preposterous, though showing what accomplished horsemen they were,[1]

---

[1]Though it may seem hard to believe, the writer has seen a Mexican, for exhibition in a race of some length, transfer himself from

they undertook to change from one saddle to the other. It is needless to say that the attempt came to grief, as at the critical moment, when neither was seated, a sudden swelling of the flood carried both off their standing and forced them to swim to shore. The horses were swept away and probably came to an anchorage under the bluffs. They had to cast about to make a fire and dry their clothes. Then in their buckskin breeches, fitting torturously tight, they tracked it home on foot, where they had to relate their rash adventure. Hence the tale and the moral:

"Do not swap horses in crossing the stream."

Plow Around the Log.

The absolute newness of military con-

---

one saddle to another without halt. The question being put to him in relation to this tale. "Leon, could *you* swap saddles in a flood?" He stoutly responded, not knowing the joke: "If it did not come over the bow to make the seat slippery, why—*certero! cert!*"

scription in the United States and the indefatigable attempts of nearly all concerned to avoid their obligations gave rise to many contentions. A State governor, charged with his con-citizens' grievances and his own consequent embarrassments, rushed to Secretary Stanton and was received in a manner quite in accordance with that official's overbearing character; thereupon he hastened to the President to rehearse his reception as an additional matter to be remedied. To the amazement of a friend he came from a three hours' interview appeased, and departed smilingly for home.

His introductor no sooner saw the Chief than he eagerly inquired by what concessions he had pacified the irritated governor and sent him away in good humor.

"Oh, I did not concede anything," explained the President. "You know how the Illinois farmer managed the big log that lay in the middle of his field? To the inquiries of his neighbors one Sunday, he responded that he had got rid of the big log.

" 'How ever did you do it? It was too big to haul away, too knotty to split, too wet and soggy to burn; how ever did you do it?'

" 'Well, now, boys,' said the farmer, 'if you won't tell the secret, I 'll tell you how. I just plowed around it.'

"Now," said Lincoln to the questioner, "don't tell anybody, but I just 'plowed around' the governor. But it took me three mortal hours to do it, and I was afraid every minute that he would see what I was at."

Related by General J. B. Fry.

"I will Risk the Dictatorship."

"I have placed you at the head of the Army of the Potomac. . . I have heard . . . of your recently saying that both the army and the Government needed a dictator. Of course it was not for this, but in spite of it, that I have given you the command. . . What I now ask of you is military success, and I will risk the dictatorship!"

Letter to General Hooker, Jan., 1863.

Still Heard From.

In the fall of 1863, when General Burnside had penetrated so far within the enemy's lines in Tennessee that his situation was regarded as critical, a telegram reached headquarters stating that "firing was heard towards Knoxville."

"I am glad of it!" exclaimed the President. Asked the cause of his gladness, he returned: "Because I am reminded of Mrs. Sallie Ward, a neighbor of mine, who had a large family. Occasionally, one of her numerous progeny would be heard crying from some out-of-the-way place, upon which Mrs. Ward would exclaim:

"'Thank the Lord, there's *one* of my children is n't dead yet.'"

Nobility Not a Bar in our Army.

A foreign officer who tendered his services to the country, and was promised a commission, thought it a clincher to announce that he had other than military claims to the favor, and mentioned his letter of nobility.

"Oh, never mind," said the President, "you will find *that* no obstacle to your advancement."

"Take the People into our Confidence."

In 1863, President Lincoln had full powers and was as nearly an autocrat as a constitutional ruler could be; but as far as possible, he in no way relaxed the frank and neighborly manner which he had imported from the free-and-easy West. A reporter once stated that he had been invited to attend a meeting of the war governors in Washington, and that the President had sanctioned the invitation. But at the meeting one of the officials objected to the presence of an "outsider" and the reporter was making off when Lincoln intervened.

"Wait a minute, young man," said he, and then explained that he had consented to his being present—"for I don't intend to say anything to-day that is secret in any sense," he continued, "and I thought we might just as well take the people into our confidence. However, it is for you gentlemen to say."

The position had become so uncomfortable for the newspaper man that he bowed himself out. He never knew what further was said about it, but that night Governor Buckingham gave him a report of the meeting.

Better Say Nothing.

At the opening of the war and during its progress, the national weakness for speeches on all occasions became a positive burden to public men, particularly as audiences always expected a speaker to be equipped with a full quiver of apposite remarks. It was truly said of the President that "*Abundat dulcibus vitiis* (He abounds in pleasant thoughts)," but he knew also when to be silent. At one time in 1863, when all the prominent personages were called upon to make speeches, Lincoln at his turn sensibly said:

"I appear before you, fellow-citizens, merely to thank you for this compliment. The inference is a very fair one that you would hear me for a little while at least, were I to commence to make a speech. I do not appear before you for the purpose of doing so, and for several substantial reasons. The most substantial of these is that I have no speech to make. In my position it is somewhat important that I should not say any foolish things. [A voice, 'If you can help it.'] It very often happens that the only way to help it is to say nothing at all. Believing that is my present condition this evening, I must beg of you to excuse me from addressing you further."

A Trenchant Stroke of Wit.

Under the most severe strain, the President most invariably had recourse to humor. His rival, for a time, for popularity, General McClellan, was pronounced by him frankly "a pleasant and scholarly gentleman." Before being forced to remove him, for the failure of his "scholarly" plans to fruit, Lincoln said: "If the General has no use for the Army of the Potomac I should like to *borrow* it for a little while." When the same General, developing political prudence, kept silence in regard to the campaign paper known as "the Chicago Letter," Lincoln gave, as a reason, that the advocate of the spade and pick—McClellan was an engineer officer by training—was "entrenching."

"Paint Me With the Wart."

When the Lord Protector of England sat for his likeness to Cooper, an eminent painter of the time, he protested on finding that the artist was going to draw him in profile:

"No, a full face—paint me with the wart!"

In an equally frank way, though with his gentle irony, President Lincoln said to the portrait painter, Mr. Frank Carpenter:

"Do you think you *can* make a handsome picture of *me?*"

"A General, at Last."

During the war the most indulgent critic of the military movements could not refrain from laughing at the long-drawn-out pageant of commanders in the Virginia Valley, from "Old Fuss-and-feathers"—for even age and proven talent did not save General Scott, the patriarch-general, from the American propensity to bestow nicknames upon their servitors, as the Romans gave crowns to theirs—to the "great arithmeticians who had never set a squadron in the field," much less handled an army of defence. When the Western Marius (New Carthage had fallen to his arms) reached Washington, he was a disappointment—the taciturn, cigar-smoking, statuesque Grant, who "promised no reviews for the amusement of the Washington ladies and no 'show business.'"

He had a private interview with the President, of which he has given an account in his *Memoirs*. At its close, Lincoln said to an inquirer:

"Thank God, we have a General, at last!"

Do Not Break, but Hold On!

"I have seen your despatch expressing your unwillingness to break your hold. Neither am I willing. Hold on with a bull-dog grip."

President Lincoln to General Grant, August, 1863.

"Government Of the People, By the People, and For the People, Shall Not Perish!"

"Four-score and seven years ago our fathers brought forth upon this continent a new nation, conceived in liberty, and dedicated to the proposition that all men are created equal. Now we are engaged in a great civil war, testing whether that nation, or any nation so conceived and so dedicated, can long endure. We are met on a great battle-field of that war. We have come to dedicate a portion of that field as a final resting place for those who here gave their lives that that nation might live. It is altogether fitting and proper that we should do this. But in a larger sense we cannot dedicate, we cannot consecrate, we cannot hallow this ground. The brave men, living and dead, who struggled here have consecrated it far above our power to add or detract. The world will little note, nor long remember, what we say here, but it can never forget what they did here. It is for us, the living, rather to be dedicated here to the unfinished work which they who fought here have thus far so nobly advanced. It is rather for us to be here dedicated to the great task remaining before us, that from these honored dead we take increased devotion to that cause for which they gave the last full measure of devotion; that we here highly resolve that these dead shall not have died in vain; that this nation, under God, shall have a new birth of freedom, and THAT GOVERNMENT OF THE PEOPLE, BY THE PEOPLE, AND FOR THE PEOPLE, shall not perish from the earth."

Address, dedicating the National Cemetery at Gettysburg, Nov. 19, 1863.

This speech contains but 266 words. According to Edward Everett[1] it eclipsed his own elaborate oration on the same

[1] Edward Everett was deemed at the time the foremost orator of the country.

occasion. It was read from a few sheets of foolscap, but was the result of four or five essays to reach perfection. It lasted five minutes—and will live forever. Unwittingly it was a verbal duel between colloquial and literary language.

For a Soldiers' Cemetery.

On visiting the cemetery of the Soldiers' Home in Washington, the President said:

" 'How sleep the brave who sink to rest
By all their country's wishes blest!
. . . .
And women o'er the graves shall weep,
Where nameless heroes calmly sleep.' "

All Hands and No Mouths.

"I hold that if the Almighty had ever made a set of men that should do all the eating and none of the work, He would have made them with mouths only and no hands; and if He had ever made another class that He intended should do all the work and no eating, He would have made them with hands only and no mouths."

On the Women in the War.

"I have never studied the art of paying compliments to women; but I must say that, if all that has been said by orators and poets, since the creation of the world, in praise of women, were applied to the women of America, it would not do them justice for their conduct during this war. God bless the women of America!"

At a Soldiers' Fair, at Washington, 186—.

"The Handsomest Man."

A mother had obtained the pardon for her son, condemned by a court-martial, through personal intercession with the President. Her explanations justified giving the pardon. On leaving the room, she broke out:

"I knew it was a 'Copperhead' lie! Why, they told me that Mr. Lincoln was an ugly-looking man, and it is a lie. He is the handsomest man I ever saw in my life."

The glow of goodness had transfigured him, as has been noticed in other instances.

By Thaddeus Stevens, the intercessor in question.

The Pact with Divinity.

The Emancipation Proclamation was issued New Year's day, 1863. In the preceding September the Confederates had been defeated at the battle of Antietam. Lincoln presented his draft of the proclamation at the next Cabinet meeting, where he made the statement that he had made a solemn vow before God, that if General Lee were driven back from Pennsylvania he would crown the result by the declaration of freedom to the slave.

On signing the document he remarked:

"This signature will be closely examined and if they find that my hand trembled they will say that I hesitated or was irresolute. But," continued the author of that noblest gift to the negro, "it is not because of any uncertainty or hesitancy on my part—only [it was after the New Year public reception], three hours' handshaking is not calculated to improve a man's chirography."

"It Is My Object to Break up that Game."

In September, 1863, a peculiar kind of sedition seethed in the army before Washington. It was stated to President Lincoln that a Major Key, on General McClellan's staff, had replied to a brother officer that "the game was to exhaust both armies by fruitless operations so that a compromise could be effected and slavery, as an institution, saved."

Summoned before the President, as his chief, the Major did not deny his words or their substance, but . protested his loyalty.

The judge said: "Gentlemen, if there is a 'game,' even among Union men, not to have our army take any advantage of the enemy it can, it is my object to break up that game."

The offender was cashiered, and Lincoln privately commented:

"Dismissed, because I thought his silly, treasonable expressions were 'staff talk,' and I wished to make an example."

"I Can Bear Censure, but Not Insult."

A cashiered officer persisted several times in presenting to the President a plea for his reinstatement, and was finally assured that even his own statement did not justify a rehearing. His final application being met with silence he lost temper and blurted out:

"Well, Mr. President, I see that you are fully determined not to do me justice."

Without evincing any emotion Mr. Lincoln rose, laid some papers on the desk, and suddenly seizing the officer by the coat-collar, marched him to the door. After ejecting him into the hall, he said:

"Sir, I give you fair warning never to show yourself here again! I can bear censure, but not insult."

To the Army and the Navy.

Nothing more plainly and loudly proclaims the modesty of Lincoln than his eulogy of the Army and Navy when he publicly expressed his gratitude without taking one laurel-leaf to himself. What a contrast to the vainglorious bulletins of Napoleon.

Lincoln's Tribute to the U. S. Army: "No part of the honor for the plan or the execution [of the ending of the Rebellion] is mine. To General Grant, his skilful officers and brave men, it all belongs." 1865.

Lincoln's Tribute to the U. S. Navy: In a paper dated 1864, intended to be read at a sailors' fair at Baltimore, he commended the navy for its great services and efficiency.

For Readiness in Emergency, Work for a Living.

By the see-saw of fortune, the victories in the West, in 1863, counterbalanced the defeats in the East. Among the conspicuous generals rose General Garfield, who executed feats in reinforcing, bringing up needed supplies, and a daring ride, worthy to be bracketed with General Sheridan's.

Lincoln asked of a *regular* army officer how it was that an amateur, like Garfield, should accomplish in two weeks what a trained officer would have wanted two months to effect.

"Because he was not educated at West Point," was the satirical reply.

"No, that is not the reason. It is because, when Garfield was a boy, he had to work for a living."

Trust the Poor.

"No men living are more worthy to be trusted than those who toil up from poverty; none less inclined to take or touch aught which they have not honestly earned."

Set your Feet Right, and then Stand Firm!

One day when Lincoln was escorting two ladies to the Soldiers' Home they were all compelled to leave the carriage, owing to the bad condition of the road due to excessive rain. Mr. Lincoln placed three stones for stepping-stones from the curb to the vehicle. While assisting the ladies to firm land, he remarked:

"All through life, be sure you put your feet in the right place, and then stand firm!"

"Keep Faith with Friend and Foe."

"There have been men base enough

to propose to me to return to slavery our black warriors of Port Hudson and Olustee, and thus win the respect of the masters they fought. Should I do so, I should deserve to be damned in time and eternity. Come what will, I will keep my faith with friend and foe."

On July 30, 1863, the President issued an Executive order placing black soldiers on an equality with white. Unfortunately, the Secretary of War contravened this with an order of his own, which caused a confusion unhappy both for the colored soldiers and for the captured rebels, who were held man for man and treated precisely as were the black prisoners by the Confederates—that is, restored to the conditions during slavery. Previously, a cartel had allowed exchange without recognizing the rebels as belligerents. Later, when there was the large number of captives from Vicksburg, etc., Stanton refused to exchange, because it would reenforce the failing cause with sound men.

General Grant finally compelled the strict military rule to be complied with regardless of politics or policy. But the colored soldiers suffered more than the white ones. President Lincoln spoke the above words to some Western visitors on the definite repeal of the Fugitive Slave Law in 1864.

Go Home and Raise the Men!

It has long been asserted, and it is fairly proved, that the first nomination of Abraham Lincoln for President, and the determined prevention of his being shelved into the candidacy for Vice-President in 1860, was due to a concerted and well-matured plan elaborated by Mr. Medill of the Chicago *Tribune,* and by other writers and politicians of Illinois. This seems to be borne out by Mr. Medill's account of an interview with the President in 1864. The call for more troops revolted the citizens of Chicago. Medill went with a deputation of Cook County citizens to demand a reduction of its quota. They argued in vain with Secretary Stanton and with General James B. Fry in the President's hearing. The question was finally referred to him.

Mr. Medill relates that:

"He suddenly lifted his head and turned on us a black and frowning face.

"'Gentlemen,' he said in a voice full of bitterness, 'after Boston, Chicago has been the chief instrument of bringing the war upon this country. . . It is you who are largely responsible for making blood flow as it has. You called for war until we had it. You called for emancipation, and I have given it to you. Whatever you have asked, you have had.

"Now you come here, begging to be let off from the call for men which I have made to carry out the war *you* demanded. You ought to be ashamed of yourselves! Go home, and raise your six thousand extra men! Go home, and send us those men!'"

Abashed, they returned home—but raised and sent the men.

Going Down with Colors Flying.

It was considered very injudicious, politically, that almost coincident with Lincoln's renomination for President he should issue a call for 500,000 more men. The Cabinet officers were mouthpieces for the objections.

"Gentlemen," replied the President, "it is not necessary that I should be reelected, but it is necessary that our brave boys should be supported and the country saved. If I go down under this measure, I will go down like the *Cumberland* [1] with my colors flying."

---

[1] The U. S. Ships *Congress* and *Cumberland* were sunk by the Confederate ram *Merrimac*, March, 1862.

"With a Brave Army and a Just Cause—"

"Not expecting to see you again . . . I wish to express . . . my entire satisfaction with what you have done up to this time . . . And now, with a brave army and a just cause, may God sustain you!"

[*Letter* of the President to General Grant, April 30, 1864.],

The Solemn Pride of Patriotic Sacrifice.

Executive Mansion, Washington,
Nov. 21, 1864.

MRS. BIXBY, Boston, Mass.

DEAR MADAM:—I have been shown in the files of the War Department a statement of the Adjutant-General of Massachusetts that you are the mother of five sons who have died gloriously on the field of battle. I feel how weak and fruitless must be any words of mine which should attempt to beguile you from the grief of a loss so overwhelming. But I cannot refrain from tendering to you the consolation that may be found in the thanks of the Republic they died to save. I pray that our Heavenly Father may assuage the anguish of your bereavement, and leave you only the cherished memory of the loved and lost, and the solemn pride that must be yours to have laid so costly a sacrifice upon the altar of freedom.

Yours very sincerely and respectfully,

ABRAHAM LINCOLN.

"I Want to See Her Spread Herself!"

During the civil struggle, the agitation in Washington, which was almost beleaguered, found vent in animated discussions, and, even in the White House, where the importance of the chief's repose should have preserved decorum, the ushers and guardians assembled in their waiting room to wrangle and debate. The paited President had issued special instructions to stop these sessions, but they were unheeded from pure need of doing something to break the tension of waiting. One evening, the amateur congress was assembled, discussing the news and the more plentiful rumors, when they were amazed by the unannounced entrance of the President in his stockinged feet, unceremoniously carrying his shoes in his hand. The hubbub had helped him in his attempted stealthiness, for he was not a fairy-light walker. At the apparition of this " lean and slippered Pantaloon," the meeting promptly dissolved, the members seeming to melt away. Their dean alone stayed, the senior usher, Pendel,[1] Mr. Lincoln's own appointee whom he prized for his kindness to his children. The disturbed master shook his long bony finger at him and said:

[1] Mr. Thomas F. Pendel, usher specially appointed by President Lincoln in 1864, and in service in 1900.

"Pendel, you people remind me of the boy who set forty-three eggs under a hen. He then rushed indoors and told his mother what he had done.

"'But a hen cannot set on forty-three eggs,' remonstrated his mother.

"'No, I guess not; but I just want to see her *spread herself!*'

"That 's what I wanted to see you boys do, when I came in and caught you transgressing," concluded the President, as he returned to his own apartment.

Shape Words to Turn to Men and Guns.

In excusing himself from attending a mass meeting in New York in honor of General Grant, whose line of victories was beginning to point to the final one, the President wrote:

"Grant and his brave soldiers are now in the midst of their great trial; and I trust that, at your meeting, you will so shape your good words that they may turn to men and guns moving to his and their support."

"Civil and Political Equality to Both Races."

"The restoration of the rebel States to the Union must rest upon the principle of civil and political equality of both races; and it must be sealed by general amnesty."

[*Letter* to General Wadsworth, 1864.]

"Take the Responsibility and Act."

General Grant himself relates that when the President invested the general from the West with the rank of Lieutenant-General he stated that "all he wanted or ever had wanted was some one who would take the responsibility and act."

March 12, 1864.

The Work a Duty—the Gratitude to God.

To a deputation of the Christian Commission, testifying to the debt they owed him, Lincoln said:

"My friends, you owe me no gratitude for what I have done; and I, I may say, owe you no gratitude for what you have done; just as, in a sense, we owe no gratitude to the men who fought our battles for us. I trust that this has been for us all a work of duty. All the gratitude is due to the great Giver of all good."

"Got 'Em, for the Third Time!"

As the end of the Civil War approached, the capital was repeatedly thrilled by reports that "the backbone of the Rebellion" was broken at last. On hearing these rumors the President would only shrug one shoulder which, like a printer's, was higher than the other, and murmur:

"'Got 'em again, for the third time!'"

He was reminded, he said, of a little incident which had occurred about 1820, and which was for years the talk of the neighborhood in Fulton County, Ill. The Spoon River is one of the typical streams of the Mid-West. At times the water is high enough to float an ocean steamer "e'ena'most," and at others so low that the bed can easily be traced. It once happened that a little steamboat named the *Utility* left the Illinois River and, by some blunder, got into the Spoon, then running bank high. The nearest steamboat landing was at Havana, in Mason County, several miles from Lewistown, so the Fulton County folks were not accustomed to the sight of such craft, and the idea of a steamboat getting up the Spoon was not even dreamed of. One spring night the people heard strange and fearful sounds rising above the roaring of the waters of the freshets; they turned out of doors and stared with surprise to see, over the tree tops, a vessel spouting pitchpine smoke and flame, while the whistling was prodigious and uncanny. One of the old settlers, Sam Jenkins, had been carousing for a week, and it was "about the season for him to see things." When he heard this terrible noise he staggered out of doors and spying the monster, looking like Vesuvius afloat, he threw up his palsied hands and yelled:

"Boys, I have got 'em again, for the third time!"

The river, capricious as ever, dropped suddenly from under the adventurous craft, so unhappily attracted to that point by the congenial name of Fulton, and left it high and dry on a sand bank. The ingenious proprietor landed her machinery and with it set up a saw-mill. The cabin furniture was disposed of in the neighborhood, and one Davidson, Sheriff of Fulton County, bought the shabby little rocking chair. Some years later, during a political campaign the political leader of the region, "Uncle Nat" Beadles, was unable to offer his customary hospitality to the Democratic mouthpiece, Stephen A. Douglas, and it chanced that not only he, but Lincoln, also then a struggling law student, and the noted itinerant preacher Cartwright, also a candidate, had to sleep on soft feather ticks laid on the slab or puncheon floor of the Davidson cabin. Lincoln rocked to and fro in the rude rocking chair, and naturally was much amused by the story attached to it.

"I Count for Something!"

In 1864, Louis Napoleon III. foisted the Archduke Maximilian of Austria upon the Mexican republic as Emperor. Some of the Confederates talked of falling into rank with their Federal foes, to oust the foreigner, and this front of the Americans, combined with the determined resentment of the Mexicans, compelled the intriguing French Emperor to abandon his brother Cæsar, in 1867. Maximilian was then captured and shot by the natives. Sounded by a French notable, as to the status between France and the United States at the climax of this crowned filibustering, Lincoln replied:

"There has been war enough. I know what the American people want; but, thank God! I count for something, and during my second term there will be no more fighting."

One of the first orders of Andrew Johnson, on his untimely accession to the Chair, in 1865, accelerated the downfall of Maximilian.

A Knock-Down Argument.

A private soldier had knocked down his captain, and a court-martial had sentenced him to the Dry Tortugas. His friends bestirred themselves in his behalf, and prevailed upon Judge Schofield, a personal friend of President Lincoln, to intercede in his behalf. Lincoln paid close attention to all that Schofield had to offer, and then said:

"I tell you, Judge, you go right down to the Capitol, and get Congress to pass an act authorizing a private soldier to knock down his captain. Then come back here and I will pardon your man." The Judge saw the point, and withdrew.

"I Am the Longest, but McClellan Is Better-Looking."

An officer, on duty at Baltimore, attended a Democratic meeting and made a speech for General McClellan, who was then highly popular and a candidate for the coming Presidential election which gave Lincoln his second term. The Secretary of War suspended the officer, who thereupon presented himself to the President for reinstatement.

"When the military duties of an officer are fairly and faithfully performed," pronounced the arbiter, "he can manage his politics in his own way.[1] We have no more to do with that than with his religion. . . Supporting General McClellan is no violation of army regulations, and, as a question of taste, choosing between him and me—well, I am the *longest,* but McClellan *is* better-looking."

Veniam Petimus Damusque Vicissim. (Horace).

When two Confederate agents in Canada, Thompson and Sanders, desiring to return home, craved permission of Secretary of War Stanton to pass through the Northern States, Lincoln gave the pass in these words:

"Let us close our eyes and let them pass unnoticed."

---

[1] As Lincoln did not, in his days of military autocracy, pretend to any military knowledge, his inconsistency with tradition is pardonable, but the time-honored rule is Scriptural: "No man that warreth entangleth himself with the affairs of this life." (*Second Epistle of Paul to Timothy*, ii, 4.)

They Ought to Know.

Towards the close of the great conflict, surmises upon the length of time to which the war might be protracted were based on estimates of the hostile strength. On being asked point blank what he thought were the forces of the Confederates, the President replied offhand:

"The Confederates have some 1,200,000 in the field."

"Is it possible! how did you find that out?"

"Why," said Lincoln, "every Union general I ever heard tell—when he has been 'licked'—says the rebels outnumbered him three or four to one; now, we have at the present time about 400,000 men, and three times that number would be 1,200,000, would n't it?"

The Bible—the Best Gift to Man.

"It [the Bible] is the best gift which God has ever given to man. All the good from the Saviour of the world is communicated to us through this book. But for that book, we could not know right from wrong. All those truths desirable for men are contained in it."

On the presentation of a Bible to the President by the colored people of Baltimore, July 4, 1864.

The Cave of Adullam.

After Lincoln was renominated in 1864 General Frémont, who, because of a grievance, had resigned from the army, also ran for the Presidency. An interlocutor having referred to his strength, the President opened the Bible at the First Book of Samuel, and read:

"And every one in distress and in debt, and discontented, gathered themselves unto him, and he became captain over them, and there were with him about four hundred men."

A Little Man for a Big Business.

At the second inauguration of President Lincoln, in 1865, there was pointed out to him a famous little lad who played in the band of the Germantown Hospital as post drummer, Harry W. Stowman, aged eleven, "the Infant Drummer" of various theatrical advertisements. The President was always fond of children—but then, what that is good was he not fond of?—and had the prodigy brought to him. He caught the little fellow up in his arms and, kissing him, said:

"You are a very little man to be in this big war business."

(The editor well remembers "the Infant Drummer." He was a standing attraction in the theatre at Barnum's Museum, New York City, called "the lecture room," in order not to offend the *unco guid*. When a tune was being played by the band he would execute a drum solo which went far to confirm the opinion of a certain German drum performer, who esteemed it the greatest of musical instruments. How his little hands could get so great a volume of sound out of the hollow sphere still remains a mystery.)

Slipping down Unbeknownst.

After the capitulation of General Lee, in April, 1865, the members of the Confederate Cabinet scattered in all Southern directions. General Wilson, to whom Macon had surrendered, was chasing the President of the ex-Confederate States, who had not a last ditch for hiding. He asked for instructions in the dilemma—should he capture the fugitive or let him escape? Grant referred in person to his Chief, who said:

"This reminds me of a story:

"There was once an Irishman who had signed a Father Mathews's temperance pledge. A few days later, he became terribly thirsty, and finally applied to a bartender in a saloon for a glass of lemonade; and while it was being mixed, leaned over and whispered to him:

"'An' could n't yees put a little whiskey into it, all unbeknownst to mesilf?'

"Now, General, if Jeff can get away *unbeknownst* to us, I shall be glad."

Pluck a Thistle and Plant a Flower.

In the spring of 1865, a number of men who had resisted the draft in western Pennsylvania were pardoned in a batch, by the President. His friend Mr. J. H. Speed, who had heard the touching pleas of two women petitioners in the case, observed that he wondered why the President stood the anguish of such pleadings when he was, at heart, so sensitive.

"I have, in that order," said Lincoln, "made people happy and alleviated the distress of many a poor soul whom I never expect to see. Speed, die when I may, I want it said of me by those who know me best, that I always plucked a thistle and planted a flower, when I thought a flower would grow."

America the Treasury of the World.

"Tell the miners from me that their prosperity is the prosperity of the nation; and we shall prove that we are indeed the treasury of the world."

President Lincoln to Schuyler Colfax, April, 1865.

The Grip of an Honest Man.

During the Civil War, Lord X—— made himself notorious by his persistent support of the lost cause, in spite of the Queen's imposition of neutrality upon her subjects. He upheld the building of privateers on the Mersey, the attempts to float the cotton loan in Lombard Street, and the frenetic *canards* in the hostile press. Notwithstanding this conduct, when the last shot was fired, he presented himself at the White House to participate in the public reception, and to receive one of the hearty hand-shakes for which the President was famed. The host knew all about this alien supporter of the Confederacy, but with his most affable smile he extended his hand to the one eagerly advanced. It was without any warning, however, unless his conscience misgave him, that the Briton felt his knuckles crushed together in the Herculean grip. The disabled nobleman withdrew his hand as quickly as possible and soon withdrew in person, greatly to the amusement of those who suspected the effective punishment given by the Eagle's talon.

The Lincoln Grip.

It was remarked with wonder that at the end of the public receptions in the Executive Mansion, when all the world could clasp the President's hand, he would respond as forcibly to the last comer as to the first. Questioned upon this singular fact, Lincoln explained:

"The hardships of my early life gave me strong muscles."

Fooling the People.

"You may fool all of the people some of the time, and some of the people all of the time; but you cannot fool all of the people all of the time."

The Lord's Judgments are True and Righteous.

"Fondly do we hope, fervently do we pray, that this mighty scourge of war may speedily pass away. Yet if God will that it continue until all the wealth piled by the bondman's two hundred and fifty years of unrequited toil shall be sunk, and until every drop of blood drawn with the lash shall be paid by another drawn with the sword; as was said three thousand years ago, so still it must be said, 'The judgments of the Lord are true and righteous altogether.'"

Second Inaugural Address, 1865.

"Let Us Judge Not Lest We Be Judged."

This was the sacred text with which Lincoln rebuked the persons who clamored "We'll hang Jeff Davis to a sour apple tree!" when the ex-President of the crushed Southern Confederacy was captured at Irwinsville, Ga., after the fall of Macon.

Divination by the Bible.

On the second inauguration day of Abraham Lincoln, March 4, 1865, the gentleman who handed the Bible to the twice-chosen advocate of the people noted the place where the open book was kissed. The passage denoted, according to the hallowed *Sortes Bibliæ,* the speedy quelling of the Rebellion, namely, Isaiah v., 26, 27:

"And he will lift up an ensign to the nations from far, and will hiss unto them from the end of the earth; and behold, they shall come with speed swiftly;" and so on.

The Modern Prometheus.

In a conversation with Senator Clark (N. H.) the President observed of office-seekers:

"It seems as if every visitor darted at me, and with finger and thumb carried off a portion of my vitality! Of twenty applicants, I make nineteen enemies!"

Seven Eighths Living on the Other Eighth.

The Tite Barnacles in our midst were thus characterized by Lincoln:

"Sitting here [in the White House],

where all the avenues of public patronage come together in a knot, it does seem to me that our people are fast approaching the point where it can be said that seven eighths of them are trying to find out how they may live at the expense of the other eighth."

To Senator Clark (N. H.), 1865.

"Love Thine Enemies!"

The Marquis of Chambrun, who was in the Presidential party on a trip outside the capital, as they neared the city on their return, heard Mrs. Lincoln observe with bitterness:

"That city is filled with our enemies!"

Her husband promptly reproved her, saying:

"Enough! we must never speak of that!"

Saturday, April 9, 1865.

About the same time, when guiding the President through the Washington hospitals, Dr. Jerome Walker, of Brooklyn, turned him from a ward containing prisoners, saying:

"They are rebels."

Wherepon he was corrected with the words:

"You mean they are Confederates."

The Vast Future for America.

"There are already among us those who, if the Union be preserved, will live to see it contain two hundred and fifty millions of population. The struggle of to-day is not altogether for to-day; it is for a vast future also."

Lincoln's Last Act Was of Grace.

It was the afternoon of the mournful day of April 14, 1865.

A senator called at the Executive Mansion to confer with the President, to whom news was pouring in that might make him take back his lugubrious saying that "he would never know peace again." The Senator was J. B. Henderson of Missouri, and he was speaking in behalf of one Vaughn, a soldier in the regiment of Colonel Green of the Confederate Army. When the cause was lost Colonel Green had instructed this soldier to carry letters to his family. The courier was captured, tried and sentenced as a spy, and despite two re-trials was under the shadow of the death penalty. The President listened to the suitor, who pointed out that at last the war was decidedly at an end:

"This pardon, therefore, should be granted in the interest of peace and conciliation."

The President fully agreed and said:

"Go to Stanton and tell him this man must be released."

But the Secretary of War, who often persisted in his opposition to his chief, was violently incensed and more than usually obdurate. When the repulsed advocate returned empty-handed to the

President, the latter was dressed for the visit to Ford's Theatre. At once he wrote an order to the same effect as his verbal message, saying to Mr. Henderson:

"I think this will have precedence over Stanton!"

It was an unconditional release and pardon—the last official act of the President was one of grace. Cromwell said on his death-bed: "If once in grace is always in grace, then am I safe!"

		Order Number
Coleridge.	Rime of the Ancient Mariner	16
Concerning Friendship		85
Curtis.	Our Best Society	4
De Quincey.	Three Essays	63
Dickens.	Christmas Carol	43
	Cricket on the Hearth	44
Drake.	Culprit Fay	3
Edgeworth.	Castle Rackrent, etc.	78
Epictetus		20
Ferguson.	Father Tom and the Pope	48
Fouqué.	Sintram	76
	Undine	84
Franklin.	Autobiography	41
	Poor Richard	42
Gaskell.	Cranford	33
Gesta Romanorum		65
Gilbert.	Bab Ballads. 2 vols.	96–97
Goldsmith.	Good Natured Man	8
	She Stoops to Conquer	14
	Vicar of Wakefield	34
Gray.	Elegy in a Country Churchyard	17
Gulliver's Voyage to Lilliput		80
Gulliver's Voyage to Brobdingnag		81
Gulliver's Voyage to Laputa		82
Gulliver's Voyage to the Houyhnhnms		83
Ideals of the Republic		30
Irving.	Bracebridge Hall. 2 vols.	121–122
	Knickerbocker's New York. 2 vols.	123–124
	Legend of Sleepy Hollow	28
	Old Christmas	75
	Rip Van Winkle	29

		ORDER NUMBER
Irving.	Sketch Book. 2 vols.	55–56
	Tales of a Traveller. 2 vols.	125–126
	The Alhambra. 2 vols.	119–120
James I. of England.	Counterblaste to Tobacco	73
Johnson.	Rasselas	36
Keats.	Endymion	87
	Eve of St. Agnes	26
Lamb.	Essays of Elia. 2 vols.	61–62
	Wit and Wisdom	38
Lover.	Barney O'Reirdon, etc.	79
Lowell.	Fable for Critics	68
Macaulay.	Lays of Ancient Rome	19
Marcus Aurelius.	Thoughts	21
Michael Angelo.	Sonnets of	53
Milton.	Areopagitica	72
	L'Allegro and Il Penseroso	11
Munchausen.	Travels	39
Omar Khayyam.	Rubaiyat	47
Ouida.	Dog of Flanders	118
Pascal.	Thoughts	89
Pater.	Child in the House	51
Penn.	Fruits of Solitude. 2 vols.	91–92
Plato.	Apology of Socrates	59
	The Phædo	60
Poe.	Gold Bug	1
	Poems	52
Rochefoucauld.	Maxims	117
Roosevelt.	True Americanism	70
Rossetti.	Blessed Damozel	45
	House of Life	18
Ruskin.	Crown of Wild Olive	88

		ORDER NUMBER
Ruskin.	Ideas of Truth	25
	King of the Golden River	27
	Sesame and Lilies	22
Shakespeare.	As You Like It	108
	Hamlet	113
	Julius Cæsar	111
	Macbeth	112
	Merchant of Venice	107
	Midsummer Night's Dream	106
	Much Ado About Nothing	105
	Romeo and Juliet	110
	Sonnets	37
	Tempest	104
	Twelfth Night	109
Sheridan.	Rivals	7
	School for Scandal	6
Stephen.	Robert Louis Stevenson	57
Stevenson.	Virginibus Puerisque	69
	Will o' the Mill	86
Tennyson.	In Memoriam	93
	Princess	50
Thackeray.	Charity and Humor	13
	Novels by Eminent Hands	32
	Rose and the Ring	23
Winthrop.	Love and Skates	49
Word for the Day		71
Zschokke.	Tales	35

G. P. Putnam's Sons
New York and London